BOUNDARIES & THRESHOLDS

Boundaries & Thresholds

Papers from a Colloquium of
The Katharine Briggs Club

Edited by Hilda Ellis Davidson

ACKNOWLEDGEMENTS

Our thanks are due to Lord Marks, whose generous grant from the Michael Marks Charitable Trust made the publication of this book possible. We are grateful too to Dr Emily Lyle, President of the Traditional Cosmology Society, for her support, and to Nancy Chambers of the Thimble Press for the lively interest she has shown in the preparation of this book, and for constant encouragement and advice.   H.D.

Boundaries and Thresholds is produced
and distributed by The Thimble Press for
The Katharine Briggs Club

Orders to
The Thimble Press, Lockwood, Station Road
Woodchester, Stroud, Glos. GL5 5EQ

Boundaries and Thresholds
First published 1993
ISBN 0 903355 41 8
Copyright © 1993 Hilda Ellis Davidson and
contributors

All rights reserved

Keyed at The Thimble Press
Typesetting by Avonset, Midsomer Norton, Bath
Printed in Great Britain by
Short Run Press, Exeter

CONTENTS

Hilda Ellis Davidson
Introduction 7

Reimund Kvideland
Establishing Borders: The Narrative Potential of a Motif 13

Alan W. Smith
Crossing the Other Line: Some Arctic Analogues of the Traditional Equator Ceremony 21

Patricia Lysaght
Bealtaine: Irish Maytime Customs and the Reaffirmation of Boundaries 28

Samuel Pyeatt Menefee
Megalithic Movement: A Study of Thresholds in Time 44

Juliette Wood
Another Island Close at Hand: The Irish Immramma and the Travelogue 54

J. R. Porter
Thresholds in the Old Testament 65

Theo Brown
Tom Pearce's Grey Mare: A Boundary Image 76

Karin Kvideland
Boundaries and the Sin-Eater 84

Ruth Richardson
Death's Door: Thresholds and Boundaries in British Funeral Customs 91

Contributors 103

Introduction

HILDA ELLIS DAVIDSON

*One more river
And that's the river of Jordan,
One more river,
There's one more river to cross.*

The concept of boundaries to be crossed and thresholds to be passed in the life of the individual and the community was first developed by Arnold van Gennep in 1908 in *Les rites de passage*. He showed how the path from birth to death was divided by a series of boundaries, and how their importance was instinctively recognized by the community. The birth of a child, entry into adult life, betrothal, marriage, parenthood, retirement and finally death are all likely to be marked by rites and ceremonies. Similarly entry into a special vocation or attainment of a new social status, as when someone becomes a monk, a knight, or a king, is felt to demand ceremonial. There may also be rites marking initiation into a limited group, ranging from a children's gang or craft apprenticeship to admittance into a secret society such as the Freemasons. Once one begins to list the rituals associated with occasions like these, the significance of the crossing of boundaries in our lives becomes apparent.

There are also the recognized boundaries of the changing seasons, marking the recurrent pattern of the solar or lunar year for the community as a whole. Thus the first of May ushering in the summer or the opening of the new year may be marked with ceremonial. Van Gennep noted too the boundaries between peace and war, plague and health, and that all-important one between sacred and profane. This may be recognized in many ways, perhaps by ceremonies at the crossing of a threshold into an area of sacred space, or by visions of ascent to the heavens or descent under the earth in order to enter a realm outside time.

Visible geographical boundaries – the frontier between states, for instance, or the point where cultivated land gives way to the wild and untamed – possess a significance far beyond their practical utility. The passions that rage over the safeguarding of boundaries even of small fields or gardens are reflected in numerous court cases and perennial battles over rights-of-way, and so it has been from the remote past. Wayland Hand (1983: 8) gives an example from North America of a way of dealing with a dispute over fencing: one claimant would put up a second boundary fence so that farm wagons could pass along the strip of disputed territory, and this was known as 'The Devil's Lane'. A similar name, 'The Devil's Gap', was used for the roadway between the church at Clare in Suffolk and the Six Bells Inn opposite the church tower, in this case a gap between sacred and profane. The area of No Man's Land between two opposing armies or the lines of trenches in the 1914-18 war are grimmer examples of this type of boundary, which Tolstoy describes in *War and Peace* as a 'terrible line of uncertainty and fear, like a line dividing the living from the dead' (II, 19).

It was pointed out by van Gennep (1960: 21) that crossing boundaries can involve preliminal rites of separation, followed by transitional rites, and ending with postliminal rites of incorporation into the new world. In some elaborate initiation ceremonies, candidates may be required to suffer pain and humiliation, perhaps even torture and mutilation in ordeals imposed upon them, while the period leading to their final acceptance in a new role may be prolonged over years. There may be a sojourn in the wilderness for those preparing to cross a crucial boundary in life; a symbolic journey may take place, such as a pilgrimage or a funeral procession from home to the place of graves, while a departure over the sea is a favourite symbol of a boundary crossing. Calendar boundaries give the opportunity to seek for omens and signs to indicate whether the next period of time will be blessed with good fortune, and these are marked not only by feasting and exchange of hospitality but sometimes by violence and mayhem, the permitted overturning of customary order during the time of transition, creating a period of confusion before normal living is restored. Participants may put on disguises, appearing as fantastic beings, strangers from another world, or as birds and animals.

One function of a boundary is to keep out enemies and protect those inside from danger, illustrated by a recorded Slav custom at a time of pestilence, when naked women dragged a plough around their village at night, cutting a deep furrow to enclose it (Hand 1983: 5). Other rites have their purpose in maintaining boundaries. The Beating of the Bounds at Rogationtide still continues in some parishes; it was practised in the Christian church from at least the sixth century, and used as a means of blessing the fields. After the Reformation Anglican clergy were encouraged to continue it, with pauses at fixed points along the route for the minister to preach or pray. George Herbert in 1652 in *The Country Parson* commends the custom which 'preserved justice in the preservation of boundaries', but the boys taking part must have viewed the practice with mixed feelings, since they were likely to be beaten, bumped, thrown into streams, dragged through hedges or made to climb over roofs in order to impress the boundary on their young minds (Hole 1978: 252). A less painful way to assist the memory, examples of which

Introduction

survive from the thirteenth century in Norway, was to recite doggerel verses cataloguing points along the boundary (Hale 1983: 183-4).

Sometimes the crossing of a boundary is irrevocable and there is no turning back; on other occasions the traveller returns, but the price may be heavy. The importance of the transitional stage before the crossing is completed is now widely recognized, largely through the work of Victor Turner, who further developed the ideas of van Gennep. The term liminality (Latin *limen*, boundary), signifying a position on the threshold of new territory, is now in general use. People undergoing initiation rites may be viewed as beings outside the community and therefore sacred, freed from normal taboos and inhibitions. They may steal with impunity, for instance, and even be compelled to get their food in this way (Davidson 1989: 14). The major calendar boundaries were times for communication with the Otherworld, and in many tales of contacts with the fairy people or meetings with the dead, these take place at Halloween, when the new year began in pre-Christian times, or at Christmas.

Similarly the area on or between borders could be a place of inspiration or enchantment. In 'Little Gidding' T.S. Eliot calls this frontier between worlds 'the intersection of the timeless moment'. An Irish seer might seek inspiration at the edge of the sea where land and water met, and other such places – the entrance to a temple, a cave, a well or a path into the forest – were places of potency and danger. The German folklorist Klein (1933) declared the crossroads to be the most magical spot in popular tradition, and the point where paths met or two or more streams came together has since early times been credited with powers of protection and healing, favoured spots of magic spells and love auguries. Crossroads were also dangerous; ghosts were seen there, witches and demons met, and there suicides were buried, while the gallows stood nearby.

Victor Turner claims that jesters, clowns, shamans and poets belong to this border realm, while it is temporarily inhabited by initiates and outlaws, who during their sojourn can enjoy a unique consciousness of unity with each other. He refers also to liminal periods of history 'when the past has lost its grip and the future has not yet put on definite shape' (Turner 1980). Concepts like these help to explain not only the long life of certain strange rites and customs, but also much religious and mythological symbolism, and memorable images found in folk and fairy tales and in great works of art. We remember from childhood the hero riding through the ring of fire, breaking through the thorn hedge to reach the enchanted princess, or climbing the tree which takes him to a realm where giants can be slain and treasure won. Memorable also is the river forded by Christian and Mr Valiant-for-Truth in Bunyan's *Pilgrim's Progress* on the last stage of the journey to the Celestial City, each struggling through deep water when his time came until 'all the Trumpets sounded for him on the other side'. There are tales of contacts across such barriers – the friendly albatross emerging from 'the realms of mist and snow' in Coleridge's *Ancient Mariner* is one – and we may find the world turned topsy-turvy, as in Ben Jonson's *Bartholomew Fair* and Shakespeare's *As You Like It* and *A Midsummer Night's Dream*, where the mentors and guides in the forest are clowns and jesters and mischievous supernatural beings.

The subject of boundaries thus seemed a good theme for a conference held by the Katharine Briggs Club at Madingley Hall near Cambridge in April 1991. The aim of this group is to bring together scholars working in different fields, particularly those which interested Katharine Briggs herself: oral tradition, ballads, tales and legends and fairy lore, together with the history and literature of the seventeenth century. The papers collected here are what Katharine herself might have called a 'sampler', giving some idea of the wide possibilities of the chosen theme.

The first papers are concerned with boundaries in the familiar world. Reimund Kvideland, out of his unrivalled knowledge of Scandinavian tales and legends, has selected a a group of stories about the placing of boundaries and the disputes which might arise from this. Such tales are found widely, because of a lively interest in local boundaries, which present a serious problem whenever men try to live as neighbours in a new area, and show an instinctive belief in their sanctity when once established.

Alan Smith deals with a boundary custom still alive today. The ceremony of 'crossing the line' at the Equator is popular and widely known, but here we have a study of a less familiar parallel in Arctic waters. The material comes mostly from accounts of voyages in whaling ships, which crossed the Arctic Circle about the beginning of May, so that May Day customs influenced the ceremonial. At the same time we have elements linked with the acceptance of newcomers into an established group, on which van Gennep laid such stress.

The importance of the May festival is brought out again by Patricia Lysaght in a paper on boundary customs connected with May Day in rural Ireland, containing much new material based on her fieldwork and on unpublished evidence from the archives in the Department of Folklore in University College, Dublin. Here the significance of local boundaries is linked with that of boundaries in time, in particular the first day of summer, which traditionally marked the opening of new seasonal activities on the farms. The importance of dairy produce to the Irish people resulted in many practices to protect milk and butter at this time against attempts to steal them by magical means. Another May Day custom, the re-establishment of existing boundaries, is still marked by the setting up of flowers and boughs at certain places.

Introduction

In Sam Menefee's paper we have another illuminating study of the link between boundaries of space and time. He deals with some of our most ancient landmarks, the megalithic monuments, and the wealth of legends concerning standing stones and stone circles said at certain times to move in their places, to circle, dance or even move down to the edge of water, threatening mortals with danger and yet offering a chance of winning treasure. Again there is departure from the norm at a boundary area, and emphasis on the time when movement takes place.

Juliette Wood discusses a different type of boundary in her study of the link between the supernatural world in popular and learned tradition and certain geographical areas in our own world, from which strange accounts were brought back by travellers. She shows the importance of such records of far-off places and peoples in medieval literature, since these have contributed to the concept of the Otherworld, and could be transformed into accounts of journeys across the barrier between sacred and profane, life and death.

The second group of papers is concerned with the crossing of such Otherworld barriers. Roy Porter's paper takes us into the remote past in his detailed discussion of the significance of the threshold in early religions of the Near East. Beginning with some curious passages from the Old Testament, he sums up the essential features of ritual concerned with gates and doorways of temples and palaces. Because of the potential danger of these boundaries, certain protective practices were felt necessary, which can be traced through archaeological finds and early inscriptions. This shows how the threshold was viewed in very early times as a place of activity and danger.

The final boundary is the one between life and death, and we are concerned with the departure of the dead in Theo Brown's paper on the well-known Devonshire song 'Widdecombe Fair'. She suggests that the Grey Mare, borrowed to take a party of men to the Fair, is really the steed carrying the dead over the border to the realm beyond. It seems that attempts to move them across the boundary have failed, since the horse collapses and they are left as unhappy ghosts haunting the moor. She has shown how a familiar source may bear a new meaning, and left us with some tantalizing problems of interpretation.

Karin Kvideland is also concerned with the departure of the dead in her study of the strange custom of sin-eating on the Welsh border, which aroused such controversy among Welsh scholars at the end of the last century. She sees it as based on a concept of boundaries, an attempt by the living to combat the threat of death by calling in an outsider to perform rites to speed the dead on his way. In the confused time after the Reformation such rites might be introduced independently of church tradition. With the departure of the spirit beyond the boundary, the community can resume the business of living and rebuild its defences.

Introduction

Finally this last crossing of the 'ultimate threshold, the Great Divide' is dealt with in Ruth Richardson's detailed account of the popular rites employed within recent times in the crucial period between death and burial. In the wealth of evidence presented here, she has been able to draw on her book published in 1988, *Death, Dissection and the Destitute*. She brings out many aspects of boundary symbolism discussed in the other papers, and indicates the value of such rituals for the bereaved. She ends with an eloquent plea not to abandon the sympolism of the crossing of the boundary when a death takes place, for we do so at our peril.

The deep significance of boundaries in the life of the individual and the community emerges from this collection of papers presented by scholars working in different disciplines. To van Gennep, the rites of passage were a means of regeneration and reintegration within society, and more recently Barbara Meyerhoff (1982: 129) has claimed that they are a means of emphasizing group values and weakening collective tensions. Like Ruth Richardson, she feels that they are more needed today than ever. Now that the importance of the interface, the marginal zone, with its rich possibilities of creative development, is being increasingly recognized, it seems that time spent considering boundary symbolism and imagery will not be time wasted.

REFERENCES

Davidson, H.R.E. 1989: 'The Training of Warriors', *Weapons and Warfare in Anglo-Saxon England*, S.C. Hawkes ed., Oxford University Committee for Archaeology, Monograph no. 21, 11-23.

Gennep, A. van 1960: *The Rites of Passage*, trans. M.B. Vizedom and G.L. Cafee, London.

Hale, C.S. 1983: 'The River Names in *Grímnsmál* 27-29', *Edda*, R.J. Glendinning and H. Bessason eds., University of Manitoba Press, 165-86.

Hand, W. 1983: 'Boundaries, Portals, and Other Magical Spots in Folklore', Katharine Briggs Lecture No. 2, Folklore Society, University College, London.

Hole, C. 1978: *A Dictionary of British Folk Customs*, 'Rogationtide'. Paladin Books, London.

Klein, A. 1933: 'Kreuzweg' in *Handwörterbuch deutsche Aberglauben*, Vol. V.

Meyerhoff, B. 1982: 'Rites of Passage: Process and Paradox', *Celebration: Studies in Festivity and Ritual*, V. Turner ed., Smithsonian Institution. Washington D.C.

Turner, V. 1980: 'Liminality and Mortality', Firestone Lecture, delivered University of Southern California.

Establishing Borders: The Narrative Potential of a Motif

REIMUND KVIDELAND

Acquisition of property and the establishment of property lines are dealt with in many legends and chronicates. These narratives are based on customary law, religious ritual, or fiction, and often on a combination of all three.

Property acquisition can be considered a transaction involving supranormal powers: the land is taken in possession from those powers through a kind of omen. An example is the tradition of the early settlers of Iceland taking possession of the new land wherever the posts of their high-seats floated ashore.

Another magical way in which land may be acquired is, for example, through hallowing the land by carrying fire around it (Strömbäck 1928, Ejdestam 1946). Property might also be appropriated illegally, for instance, by moving border stones or markers. Among farmers in Norway this was considered the worst possible crime anyone could commit; it was called 'stealing after death'. The punishment for this crime was correspondingly cruel: the perpetrator was forced to walk again after death and struggle with the border stone (Bø 1955).

In a boundary dispute, a man might also put soil from his own land into his shoes and thus swear that he was standing on his own soil. This was a false oath, and it too was punished by having to walk again after death.

Property limits might be established by a person getting as much land as he could walk or ride round or plough in one day, or as much as one could shoot or throw something across, or as far as one could carry the boundary stone, or as much as could be covered by strips from a calf skin (Ejdestam 1946).

Here I want to take a closer look at a particular legend type, namely the legend about two parties agreeing to walk towards each other at a given time, and wherever they meet would be the border between their properties. This agreement was complicated by different kinds of fraud and violence.

This legend type is known from Greek and Roman literature (Röhrich 1949-50) and from recent tradition in the Alpine region (Grafenauer 1961, Matičetov 1966 a, b), in Ireland (e.g. IFC MS vol. 238: 617-22, 305: 452-5, IFC Schools MS vol.1: 330, 333-6, 338), and in Iceland where it is connected with the division of the country into two separate bishoprics (Maurer 1861: 213 ff.). Nine Finnish variants are known, all of these contaminated, however, by the well-known legend about the wood chips floating down a river past the new settler (Siomonsuuri/Rausmaa 1968: 306 ff.). Further research has yielded fifty to sixty additional Norwegian variants and twenty Swedish variants.

The basic motif of the legend can be illustrated with the following text:

> Vårdal (in Grindheim) was to settle its borders with Spilling (in Vigmostad). Both farmers were to leave from home at sunrise; and so they met on Heddes Moor. That's where they placed the boundary stone. (Lunde 1924: 172)

What is the narrative potential the storyteller has seen in this motif for telling a suspenseful or entertaining story?

Generally speaking it is a question of conflict based on actual or suspected fraud, and the resolution of the conflict by fixing a new border. However, one or both parties may simply feel dissatisfied with the proposed solution, without giving any specific reason. More often, however, the reason for dissatisfaction is stated:

> Rauland, Ausbø and Hadland were three neighbouring farms. But between Rauland and Ausbø there were no border markings. The man on Rauland was called Rau and the man on Ausbø was called Au. These two, Rau and Au, arranged to meet one morning and where they met would be their property line. No sooner said than done, they met, but Rau thought Au had come too far, they got angry with each other and Rau killed Au and buried him in a scree. And then they are out of the legend. (NFS M. Moe 73, 24)

The storyteller has placed the event in the distant past with the original settlers as actors.

None of the legends cited so far concludes logically, that is, none of them actually explains just why the division is deemed unfair. The simplest explanation for the dissatisfaction is that one of them started walking too early. Whether the violation of the agreement is real or not is of less significance:

> The man from Breivik was arguing with an easterner about their moor pasture. The easterner's name was Skjøri. He was from Mo parish in Austland. They agreed to start walking from their respective homes at the same hour and walk at normal speed until they met. That's where the boundary was to be.
>
> But Skjøri cheated by taking off early. The man from Breivik didn't get any further than Skjøri's Moor before he met Skjøri.
>
> So he rushed at him and killed him. One can still see the grave of Skjøri on Skjøri's Moor. (Skar 1961: vol. 2, 278)

Establishing Borders

It is also possible to give a rational explanation of the fraud:

> In the old days there were often border disputes between Sirdal and Lyse. Whenever people from Sirdal and Lyse met, they'd argue and fight. Finally they decided to put an end to this conflict. At the moment of sunrise on St Olav's Day the strongest man from Lyse was to start walking from home. A champion from Sinnes in Sirdal was to do the same. Wherever they met would be the border.
>
> Now the ascent is awfully steep and rocky up from Lyse. So the man from Lyse thought: 'If I go up to Øksstøl in the evening, I'll get approximately as far as the man from Sirdal, who doesn't have to climb many of those steep hills.'
>
> No sooner said than done, and so the man from Lyse got far into Sirdal Moor before he met the man from Sirdal. They began to argue and came to blows. The legend says that the champion from Sirdal killed the man from Lyse. But he was so badly injured himself that he died there on the moor. They were both buried in Dyrgrovdalen, where the fight had taken place. Old folks still remember the spot where they lie. (*Ord og sed.* Varia 1937, I. Tjørholm)

Logically speaking this kind of cheating on an understanding should lead to a mathematically based partition. But in that case the reasoning behind the fraud would change the traditional tendency of the legend, and that is why we get no logical settlement in this instance either.

At first glance it seems that the emphasis is on the conflict itself and on the tragic end of the perpetrator of the fraud. But it only seems that way. If this were the emphasis, then it would have been natural for the *swindler* to complete his crime by killing his opponent. But that is not the case; it is almost always the victim who becomes so angry that he kills his opponent. With that he should be in a position to determine the border as he sees fit and thereby nullify the fraud, as in the following variant:

> This happened a long time ago, when there were no farms yet between Kyllingstad and Berkjeland. There were no property lines to show how much each owned. So they were going to settle the border. They agreed they'd walk from home in the morning and wherever they met there would be the line. Then the man from Kyllingstad got up so early he got almost all the way to Berkjeland. But then the man from Berkjeland got so mad he killed the Kyllingstad man and then he set the border where he wanted it himself. (EFI Hannaas 49, 7)

This variant is quite isolated, however. The reason that this motif can be employed here is that now there is no contiguous border between the two opponents, because in the meantime several other farms have been established in between.

In the tradition about border conflicts between Setesdal and Telemark, the description of the fighting is particularly dramatic. Most of the variants connect the action with Stridsmoen (Fight Moor) and nearby Skjelebekk (Border Creek):

> The people of Valle were fighting with the folk from Skafse over their border on the moors. They agreed they would walk from their respective homes at the same hour one morning and walk at normal speed. Wherever they met would be the border.
>
> But the Valle men left in the evening and came far in on the land belonging to Skafse. There they met their opponents way east of the woods and they were feeling quite cocky. 'Thank God we took off last night,' they said. But the Skafse men rushed at them and chased them back. On the moor at Lake Fyre the fight started once again. But the men from Skafse won that time too. However when they were chasing them back over the hills around Lake Fyre, a miracle happened. There came a fall of rock, and it went right between the two sides. A stream followed the landslide and it divided so prettily, one part flowing east to Lake Tjølling, the other home towards Bear Lake, that they agreed that the stream should be the borderline. So they called it Skulsbekken (Divider Stream), because it is the divider between Skafse and Valle. (Skar 1961: vol. 1, 277)

A divine judgement is a decision by supreme authority; consequently a border established by divine judgement cannot be appealed against. To argue any further becomes an impossibility. The epic limit has been reached.

In the legend, cheating on the agreement usually breeds conflict and leads to the loss of life. But logically speaking there could also be a negotiated, peaceful settlement after the deception. The motif of a negotiated settlement is found in tradition in exceptional cases. The losing party may receive certain compensations. For example, it is an alternative when one of the parties has walked all the way to the fenced-in meadow immediately surrounding the house of his opponent. Clearly that is not where the border between the two properties is, and therefore the narrator cannot place it there. He has created a dilemma he must solve in such a way that tradition and reality agree. He has several motifs at his disposal.

One motif is that the losing party chases the opponent back. Another is that the winner gives the loser another chance, for example, by letting him take a stone's throw of land. Storytellers have had difficulties integrating this motif with the traditional plot of this type of legend. I know of a single variant where it has been integrated successfully, but the collector Edvard Langset was quite aware that this variant was unusual:

Establishing Borders

This story has such a gentle and peaceful spirit. Normally this legend ends with one neighbour killing the other. (NFS Langset 13, 80-83)

In one variant of the legend about the Klungland man and the Grøtteland man, it says that when the Klungland man got angry, the Grøtteland man gave him a stone's throw. But the Klungland man still wasn't satisfied and killed the Grøtteland man. Inasmuch as the party who has come farthest is still killed, compensation remains a blind motif, that is, a motif without a real meaning.

The motif has also been coupled with the fear of oversleeping. When the man finally falls asleep, he sleeps so late that he meets his opponent on the border of his own outlying fields. He is so upset, he begs for one stone's throw into the woods, which is granted:

> Then he took a boulder and threw it so far that it didn't fall until it reached a lake halfway between Brødskjø and Ausland. In the middle of the lake one can still see the boulder sticking up from the lake which is called Rock Lake. (Riksarkivet Faye VI, 12, 39)

Here the storyteller leaves reality behind and steps into the realm of fantasy. The fantastic lies not only in the length of the throw but in the enormous dimension of the rock. This legend is comparable to the tradition about trolls throwing boulders still found as landmarks in nature.

Fantasy is given full range also in another variant, but here it is humour which dominates the clash between two brothers Nykkland and Meland:

> The Melands man got up so early he almost reached the farmhouse at Nykkland.
>
> 'Now I won't have any woods left,' said the Nykklands man. 'Can't I get back a stone's throw?' he said.
>
> 'Sure I've nothing against that,' said the other.
>
> He threw the stone almost all the way to the house of Meland.
>
> 'Oh, shit! It slipped out of my hand, otherwise I'd thrown it all the way into your yard,' he said. (Skar 1961: vol. 2, 352)

As historian Lars Reinton suggested, this motif may have some connection with ancient customary law. In his important work on Norwegian summer farming, Reinton relates the following tradition from Valdres:

> When farmers in the old days disagreed on the boundaries for their pastures on the summer farms in the mountains, it was a rule that each should own as far as he could throw a particular stone which they agreed on using for this purpose.

If this tradition is true, Reinton adds,

> then it is probably a late remnant of the medieval *snidilvarpet* [axe-throw] which was employed when someone was to appropriate part of the common. (Reinton 1961: vol. 3, 283)

According to Frostating Law (chapter 14.8) and Landsloven (National Law, chapter 7.62), *snidilvarpet* applies only to the appropriation of areas from which people obtained fence materials. The example from Valdres stands alone in recent tradition. According to Julius Ejdestam:

> It is quite clear that appropriation by stone throwing is not a rational procedure ... The act of throwing in this instance constitutes a magical practice that has developed into a legal practice, found its way into the law code and been misinterpreted. (Ejdestam 1946: 111)

A group of Swedish legends from Ångermanland closely approximates to the folktale genre. This is perhaps because they are tied to early history, near-mythical time, and to a mythical character. The story is about Gunnil Snålle (Snaela, Nålle) and how she established the borders between the provinces of Ångermanland and Jämtland. The following version is closest to the folktale (cf. AT 875 and Motif H 1050 ff.):

> In Gunnhild's time there was no definite border between the two provinces, and this caused all kinds of troubles and conflicts. Gunnhild wanted to remedy that, and so she went to the king and asked permission to settle the border.
>
> The king said neither yes nor no. First he wanted to see whether she was suitable for the job. She was to come and see him, he said, when it was neither a waxing nor a waning moon, neither day nor night, neither dressed nor naked, and neither riding nor walking. And he added that she should let him know when she was ready to come.
>
> And Gunnhild, she prepared like a real man. She waited for a time just at dawn at new moon, and she made herself a garment from a piece of fishing net. Then she took a ram and put one leg on its back but kept the other on the ground, and this way she came marching to the king. She had passed the test and got permission as desired. (Nordlander 1899: 136 ff).

We can also ask whether there are narrative possibilities which storytellers have failed to exploit.

There are two motifs especially which come to mind. One is the motif of a lawsuit or revenge after a killing, which does not occur. The reason is probably that the legends attempt to explain an existing boundary that is somehow unusual or goes back to the foundation of the farms. The

Establishing Borders

other motif is that of the walking dead. It would have been natural for the victim to walk after death at the place of the killing, but this motif is practically unknown or at least rare in Norwegian tradition.

Only in a few cases do the storytellers introduce supranormal motifs. Could it be that the story is not regarded as a true historical legend, and therefore does not need a supranormal sanction?

In many cases the legend explains an existing boundary that goes back as far as people can remember. There is no evidence that this legend has created bad feeling between the involved parties. If this had been the case, the murderer would have been deemed to walk again after death. This can also be explained by the fact that the legend accounts for an establishing of the boundary at a particular point: the rest of the boundary and the full size of the property is of no interest.

It has been my aim to present the narrative potential storytellers have seen in a simple basic motif and the various ways in which it can be developed into a story with an action and a theme. I emphasize that we are not talking about narrative development in an evolutionistic sense. Short forms and extended epic forms can exist side by side in one and the same area of tradition. It seems as if it is important for the epic formation that the motifs mirror given ecological conditions. It is the natural environment, the size of the property and the kinds of natural resources which determine the choice of additional epic motifs the storyteller grafts to the basic motif.

All the variations of this legend stress the boundary as a concrete localized point. People measure their property with their own walking, and where they meet their neighbour, they set the boundary, mark it with a boundary stone or with their own bodies and graves.

REFERENCES

Aasen, I. 1853: *Prøver af Landsmaalet i Norge*. Christiania.
Bø, O. 1955: 'Deildegasten', *Norveg* 5, 105-24. Oslo.
EFI: Etno-folkloristisk institutt. Universitetet i Bergen.
Ejdestam, J. 1946: 'Omfärd vid besittningstagande av jordegedom', *Svenska landsmål och svenskt folkliv* 69, 86-114. Uppsala.
Grafenauer, I. 1961: 'Der slowenisch-kroatisch-ladinische Anteil an der Grenzlaufsage und dessen Bedeutung', *Volkskunde in Ostalpenraum* (Alpes Orientales 2) 42-47. Graz.
Holthausen, E. 1886: *Beiträge zur vergleichende Märchen- und Sagenkunde, Germania: Vierteljahrsschrift für deutsche Altertumskunde* 31, 330 ff. Berlin.
Lunde, P. 1924: *Kynnehuset* (NFL 6). Oslo.
Matičetov, M. 1966a: 'Uno nuovo anello nelle tradizione sulla corsa per il confine', *Schweizerisches Archiv fur Volkskunde* 62, 62-76. Basel.

Matičetov, M. 1966b : 'Makedonska povedka o razmejitvenem tekn', *Folklor* 5, 1440-43. Beograde.
Maurer, K. 1861: *Isländische Volkssagen der Gegenwart*. Leipzig.
NFL: Norsk folkeminnelags skrifter. Oslo.
NFS: Norsk folkeminnesamling. Norwegian Folklore Archive. Universitetet i Oslo.
Nordlander, J. 1899: 'Hvarjehanda anteckningar', *Norrländska samlingar* 1: 4, 136 ff. Stockholm.
Orend, M. 1958: 'Vom Schwur mit Erde in den Schuhen: die Entstehung einer Sage', *Deutsches Jahrbuch für Volkskunde* 4, 386-92. Berlin.
Reinton, L. 1961: *Saeterbruket i Norge* Bd.3. Instituttet for sammenlignende kulturforskning, Serie B. Skrifter 48. Oslo.
Röhrich, L. 1949-50: 'Eine antike Grenzlaufsage und ihre neuzeitlichen Parallelen', *Würzburger Jahrbücher für die Altertumswissenschaft* 4, 339-69. Würzburg.
Siomonsuuri, L. und Pirikko-Liisa Rausmaa 1968: Finnische Volkserzählungen (Supplement-Serie zu Fabula A7). Berlin.
Skar, J. 1961-63: *Gamalt or Saetesdal*. Samla utg. 1-3. Oslo.
Strömbäck, D. 1928: 'Att helga land. Studier i landnama och det äldsta rituella besittnings-tagandet'. *Festskrift tillägnad Axel Hägerström*, 198-220. Stockholm. Reprinted Strömbäck, *Folklore och filologi*. Uppsala 1970, 135-65.

Crossing the Other Line: Some Arctic Analogues of the Traditional Equator Ceremony

ALAN W. SMITH

This paper, which is in the nature of an interim report on an investigation still in progress, has had a somewhat fortuitous origin. While collecting examples of trade initiation ceremonies I was led to Henning Henningsen's masterly volume *Crossing the Equator*, which, incidentally, covers a much wider field than its limiting title would seem to suggest. I made more specific enquiries into the general custom when writing an article for the now defunct *Sea Classic International* magazine of Summer 1986. Finally, while pursuing a quite separate line of enquiry into perceptions of the Arctic in Victorian juvenile fiction (the sort of thing sometimes irreverently referred to as 'ripping yarns'), I found still more evidence of the existence of a Northern line-crossing custom and decided that it would merit a study in its own right. Contacts with all the British and many North American maritime museums with whaling interests confirmed that no such study seemed to have been previously attempted.

Since we are dealing with a local variant of a better known and more widely practised Equator-crossing ceremony, we must first say something of the greater custom before examining the lesser.

Although the Portuguese caravels made the first regular voyages to waters south of the line, a ceremony to mark the crossing is first noted in a French source when in 1529 the Parmentier brothers 'knighted' fifty of their company and the newly made 'Chevaliers de la Ligne' were entertained to a special fish stew of bonito and albacore. From 1529 to 1666 there are, seemingly, French records only. The first English ceremony recorded was in 1670 on the Woodes Rogers voyage (Henningsen 1961: 15, 16, 84). After this, records proliferate and the custom continues into our own time.

There is no one root of this well-known and much recorded custom, and I would argue for four separate lines converging to make the ceremony we know today. Firstly, it much resembles certain forms of rough play involving ducking or splashing, for example, the traditional games called 'King Arthur' and 'Ambassador' (Grose 1981). The note on 'King Arthur' actually begins: 'A game used at sea when near the line, or in a hot latitude' and the note on 'Ambassador' begins: 'A trick to duck some ignorant fellow or landsman ... ' This logically brings us to the second strand – the initiation of newcomers or 'green hands' into the ranks of the duly qualified. There are innumerable examples of this found in shore-based occupations and it happened at sea as well. Thirdly, like so much other folk custom, crossing the line often had about it something of the nature of licensed begging or, perhaps in this case more aptly, demanding money with menaces. The ceremony could be very nasty but those favoured could pay to be let off. Fourthly, it can be seen as a vestige of ancient sacrifices deemed necessary when entering the realms of new and strange gods. There have been suggestions that both Greeks and Carthaginians performed such rites at Gibraltar (Henningsen 1961: 88).

All this can equally apply to the Arctic ceremonies which, however, also have their own specific elements. The most obvious of these is that British whalers, the source of virtually all our material, usually held their ceremony on or near May Day which roughly coincided with their crossing the Arctic Circle and/or reaching 'the country' as they called the whaling grounds. Our custom can therefore be conveniently characterized as 'the whalers' May Day'.

An early account of the essential business was published in 1827 under the heading 'Sailors on the First of May' (Hone 1827: I, cols 629-31) and runs as follows:

> Sir, You have described the ceremony adopted by our sailors, of shaving all nautical tyros on crossing the line, but perhaps you are not aware of a custom which prevails annually on the first of May, in the whale fishery at Greenland and Davis's Strait. I therefore send you an account of the celebration that took place on board the Neptune of London, in Greenland, 1824 of which ship I was surgeon at that period. Previous to the ship's leaving her port, the sailors collected from their wives, and other female friends, ribands 'for the garland' of which great care was taken until a few days previous to the first of May, when all hands were engaged in preparing the said garland, with a model of the ship.
>
> The garland was made of a hoop, taken from one of the beef casks; this hoop, decorated with ribands, was fastened to a stock of wood, of about four feet in length, and a model of the ship, prepared by the carpenter, was fastened above the hoop to the top of the stock, in such a way as to answer the purpose of a vane. The first of May arrives; the tyros were kept from between decks, and all intruders excluded while the principal performers got ready the necessary apparatus and dresses. The barber was the boatswain, the barber's mate was the cooper, and, on a piece of tarpawling, fastened to the entrance to the fore-hatchway, was the following inscription:– 'NEPTUNE'S EASY SHAVING SHOP, kept by JOHN JOHNSON.'

Crossing the Other Line

(Our source then goes on to describe the arrival of the heavily disguised celebrants on the quarter-deck where they greet the captain, wish him a prosperous fishery and accept three quarts of rum. Neptune asks whether there are any 'fresh water sailors' on board 'for, if you have, I must christen them'. The captain replies that there are eight such 'at your service' and prudently withdraws. Neptune and his court go back between decks via the forehatch from which they emerged.)

... the landsmen were ordered before Neptune, when the following dialogue took place with each ... as follows: –

Nept. What is your name? (Gilbert Nicholson.)
Where do you come from? (Shetland.)
Have you been to sea before? (No.)
Where are you going to? (Greenland.)

At each of these answers, the brush dipped in the lather (consisting of oil, tar, paint etc.) was thrust into the respondent's mouth and all over his face; then the barber's mate scratched his face with a razor, made with a piece of iron hoop well notched; his sore face was wiped with a damask towel (a boat-swab dipped in filthy water) and this ended the ceremony. When it was over they undressed themselves, the fiddle struck up, and they danced and regaled themselves with their grog until they were 'full three sheets in the wind'.

I remain, sir, etc.

H.W. Dewhurst   Crescent Street, Euston Squ.

Surgeon Dewhurst wrote his description of the custom as he saw it in 1824, and so, by a strange coincidence, did another whaler's surgeon, William Cass of the Hull vessel *Brunswick* (Credland 1988: 31-2). Cass's diary tells us that the *Brunswick* reached her whaling ground, the Davis Strait, on 8 April and then notes that

> A whimsical and ridiculous custom prevails amongst the whalers when sailing round Cape Farewell with those men who are denominated green hands or those who have never been within the Polar regions. These men are required for the benefit and diversion of their messmates to forfeit 1 lb of tobacco or an equivalent in sugar and coffee which is called a caper and to undergo the following operation ...

What follows is much as described by Dewhurst and reproduces pretty closely the Equatorial ceremony. There is a man in 'a mask and other ludicrous ornaments' as Neptune and another in female garb as his consort, here unnamed. A third principal is the Barber who 'disfigures his body to give him an appearance of corpulency' – a feature we shall find noted in another, earlier account.

We have other notices of the ceremony from the logs of that master-whaler, William Scoresby Jnr. In the first, dating from 1809 and the earliest British account yet found, Scoresby notes:

> Being now May morning the risible ceremony of putting up the garland was now performed, according to the ancient custom ...

He goes on to describe the disguised crew marching round the deck making their rough music and adds the interesting detail that it is the most recently married man of the crew who must fix the garland to the main top-gallant stay. After this, however, things are very different. Neptune does not appear at all but there is a mock fight between an elaborately costumed man 'with a hoop sword' and a hunchback wielding a deck-swab, all of which, as Cass's editor notes, is distinctly reminiscent of a mummers' play. In contrast, in his 1820 log, Scoresby records the full Neptune ceremonial with all those 'not free of the Greenland seas' being called up before him to be shaved (Credland 1988: 6).

Further descriptions can be found in the once popular works of Dr William Gordon Stables (1840-1920). Stables made a voyage to the Arctic in 1859 as one of those medical students who, seeking adventure and experience, sometimes went to sea as 'cut-price' surgeons in whalers. He graduated from Aberdeen in 1862 and then served for some years in the Royal Navy. In 1875, however, he began a new career as a writer of boys' adventure stories and historical novels. His oeuvre is extensive and not intended to be documentary, but at least twice he gives us vivid descriptions of 'the whalers' May Day'. The longest of these (Stables 1909: 70-74) is entitled 'May Day on the Pack' and begins thus:

> It may not be generally known to my readers that among the vessels that frequent the northern sea of ice the first of May is usually kept as a gala day, and the same ceremonies, with some little difference, are carried out as in ships crossing the line, although in both the custom is dying out.

The phrase 'with some little difference' is scarcely borne out by the description that follows. For one thing, the rites take place on the ice and are celebrated by a bizarre cast of characters – not only Neptune and his Lady but also Bacchus, Saturn, Ops, Jupiter, Juno and Pluto plus a gigantic bird, the Cock of the North! Five boys are duly shaved but this is said to be a preparation for a kiss from Neptune's Lady. Then the cry is raised that there are others present who have never before crossed the line. Neptune replies that they are gentlemen who have paid their footing but, at the insistence of a lady passenger, this plea is brushed aside and

Crossing the Other Line

... they were duly gowned and capped and duly shaved and kissed to the immense delight of everyone who witnessed the ceremony, especially the little boys who had been first operated on.

The second example (Stables (2): 85) is simpler and far more like a memory of things actually seen. The boy hero, Sidney Connel, is writing in his journal, the passage immediately following a description of a bloody massacre of young seals:

> Now our men – 'fine fellows' the captain calls them – are keeping May Day although it is the fifth. They haven't got a May-pole on the ice to dance round or anything like that but they have an enormous garland of artificial flowers and gay ribbons slung from a stay between the main and the mizzen. And the captain has ordered the steward to splice the mainbrace, that is, to serve out an allowance of grog to the men. They have also made themselves enormous sea-pies – potfuls in fact; and they are going to shave and duck all hands who have not crossed the Arctic Circle before. Neptune is coming aboard too, and the whole performance will be carried out just as Chips told me it is on the Equator.
>
> I don't want to be shaved and dipped, but I suppose I must submit like a man. I *am* a man!

To me this passage has about it a ring of truth, particularly in the young lad's feelings of apprehension, for the rites, whether at the line or on the Arctic Circle, could be very rough indeed and even more modern accounts (Baines 1959: 139-47) stress the terror evoked in some participants, as though the figure of Neptune, seemingly rising from the depths to challenge trespassers in his realm, struck through the irrational depths of our nature even though the rational mind *knew* he was but a shipmate disguised. Plainly in these ceremonies more than one threshold was there to be crossed.

It was by the merest chance that I happened on what seems to be the earliest record yet found of the Arctic rites. Chateaubriand went to America for the first time in 1791 and encountered 'le bonhomme Tropique' off the Banks of Newfoundland, though he did not describe this incident until he reviewed his life in his 1822 *Mémoires*. The key passage may be summarized as follows:

> The wind forced us to the north and brought us to the Banks of Newfoundland ... The men of the trident have their games which have come down to them from their ancestors: when you cross the Line, you must submit to receiving baptism ... it is the same on the Banks of Newfoundland and, whichever the place, the chief of the charade is 'the Man of the Tropic'.

This figure is described as grotesquely fat and clad in all the sheepskins and fur jackets he could lay hands on. He clambers down from the maintop where he has been lurking. Uttering hideous growls he lumbers about the deck and, seizing a bucket of water, drenches those who have never before reached the ice latitudes. Should you attempt to flee, even into the rigging, he will pursue you.

The game, our author tells us, can only be ended with a substantial tip (Chateaubriand 1822: VI, ch. 5; 'Jeux Marins').

These are but samples of a wealth of largely neglected material which is still as little known today as when Surgeon Dewhurst wrote to Hone's *Table Book* in 1827. It will be difficult to generalize about this Arctic custom because, although obviously a variant of the Equator ceremony, it has itself so many variant forms as well as appearing to have undergone a rapid evolution, as is shown by the Scoresby extracts. Where was the initiation properly practised? The Arctic Circle, the ice line, Cape Farewell? No doubt it was the older British time schedule that made the beginning of May usually coincide with crossing the Arctic line and entry into 'the country' where expectations of fame and fortune might appropriately begin with celebration and the initiation of green hands, banishing for a while thoughts of the more realistic likelihood of poverty if not death being the outcome. Northern whaling gradually fished itself out of existence and the South Sea and Antarctic fishery took its place. The new, southern whalers do not seem to have taken much notice of the old 'crossing the line' ceremony, let alone generated any new forms of their own. That Gordon Stables a hundred years ago should have declared that both tropical and Arctic customs were dying out (Stables 1909: 70) is no more than the norm for many well established folk customs. When we move away from their home territory, we too often assume that they vanished when we left.

'Crossing the Other Line' is in fact alive and well and has been recently practised in, for example, US nuclear submarines. In the midst of all their modern technology, the men of USS *Skate*, testing their boat's capacity to operate beneath – and through – the Polar ice, held initiation ceremonies for those who had never before crossed the Arctic Circle. Naturally the rites had to be modified to meet the unusual circumstances. The neophytes, wearing red-dyed long-johns, were brought before a judge, subjected to mild electric shock and had their noses painted blue (Calvert 1961: 156-7). When Commander W.R. Anderson later took USS *Nautilus* from Pacific to Atlantic under the North Pole, he does not seem to have marked the crossing of the Circle as such but did hold ceremonies at the Pole. A 'North Pole party' was held with a North Pole cake. All those present were pronounced 'Panopos' standing for 'Pacific to Atlantic via the North Pole' and

Crossing the Other Line

Father Christmas, standing in for King Neptune, made a surprise and entirely friendly visit (Anderson 1959: 225-6).

It would seem that when thresholds are encountered and new boundaries are to be crossed, custom – or should we rather say 'The wisdom of the ages'? – tells us that it is right and proper to mark the occasion with ceremonies.

REFERENCES

Anderson, W.R. 1959: *Nautilus 90° North*. Cleveland, Ohio.
Baines, F. 1959: *In Deep*. London.
Calvert, J. 1961: *Surface at the Pole*. London.
Chateaubriand, f-R. 1822: *Mémoires d'outre-tombe*. Paris.
Credland, A.G. 1988: (ed.) *The Journal of Surgeon Cass*. Hull.
Grose, F. 1981 (1911): *Dictionary of the Vulgar Tongue*. London (reprinted Illinois 1971, London 1981).
Hone, W. 1827: *The Table Book* I. London.
Henningsen, H. 1961: *Crossing the Equator*. Copenhagen.
Sea Classic International 1986: Argus Specialist Publications. Hemel Hempstead.
Stables, W.G. 1909: *From Pole to Pole*. London.
Stables, W.G. n.d. *From Greenland's Icy Mountains*. London.

Bealtaine: Irish Maytime Customs and the Reaffirmation of Boundaries

PATRICIA LYSAGHT

An astonishingly rich growth of customs has accumulated around *Bealtaine*, the May Day festival in Ireland.* Many of them focus on welcoming the summer and promoting personal and agricultural luck and prosperity. Illustrative of this is the complex of customs dealing with milk and dairy produce. As we shall see, some of these customs reflect a perception of danger at the crossing of temporal and spatial boundaries during the period of transition from spring to summer, marked by the May festival, and a need ritually to redefine and reaffirm those boundaries at this time.

In the year in Ireland *Bealtaine*, or May Day, is the boundary festival heralding the summer season. Like their Celtic forebears, the Irish divided the year into two parts: a colder period, winter, beginning at *Samhain* (1 November), alternating with a warmer period, summer, commencing at *Bealtaine* or *Cétshamhain* (1 May). *Samhain* and *Bealtaine* were major festival days signalling the beginning of these two main seasons (Rees 1961: ch. 3; MacCana 1970: 126-7).

This twofold division of the year in Ireland is well attested in early Irish literary texts. Equally well attested in these texts is the subdivision of the two major seasons of winter and summer by the festival days of *Imbolg* and *Lughnasa*. *Imbolg*, the festival of spring, divided the winter half of the year into winter and spring, and *Lughnasa*, the harvest festival, divided the summer half into summer and autumn, giving four seasons of three months each, and these remain the standard division of the year in Ireland (Lysaght 1991: 75).

Each of the four seasons was thus heralded by a major quarter-day festival marking the boundary between one season and the next (Ó Danachair 1959), and the early literary texts also offer testimony of the signficance of these days in ancient Ireland. According to these sources the great fairs or assemblies of early Ireland were held on quarter days (Joyce 1903: II, 438 ff.; MacNeill 1982: 311-49) and the same texts also stress the festive character (Meyer 1894: appendix 48-9), and the magical

---

* See evidence collected by Danaher (1972: 86-127); Buchanan (1962: 24-30) and Evans (1957: 272-4).

Bealtaine: Irish Maytime Customs . . .

connotations of the festivals (Rees 1961: ch. 3, 17). The persistence of the ancient names of three of the festivals, *Samhain, Bealtaine* and *Lughnasa* (only *Imbolg,* known as St Brigid's Day, or *Lá 'Le Bríde,* shows nominal Christianization) down the centuries (Ó Danachair 1959: 53-4), and the impressive amount of belief, custom, ritual and lore connected with them in the folk tradition of nineteenth- and twentieth-century Ireland, reminiscent of, and reflecting, far older observances, indicate that they have remained significant days in the lives of the Irish people – at least until fairly recent times.

In practical terms, *Bealtaine,* traditionally regarded as the first day of summer, was, like the other quarter days, a landmark day in the Irish countryman's calendar. Already the rigours of winter had given way to growth in spring, and now in summer nature was awake, there was renewed life in the natural environment, with trees in leaf, wild flowers in bloom, and a supply of fresh new grass for the milch cows. These could now be turned out of doors into nearby pastures, or, in communities where transhumance was still practised, sent with the dry stock to the mountain or moorland pastures since *Bealtaine* (or in some parts, *Lá Shean Bhealtaine,* Old May Day, 12 May*) marked the final departure of cattle to the mountain *buaile.* Farmers who had rough pasturage moved dry stock of sheep there from the home fields, some of which were then closed off for meadowing. Farmers might also dispose of some dry stock at this time unless they had secured additional grazing (the letting of grazing or meadowing usually dated from 1 May to 1 November), or purchase additional stock for extra grazing land rented for the 'six months term', and it was also the time when substantial graziers purchased large quantities of stock for summer pasturage; hence the prevalence and importance of May fairs, traditionally held around the beginning of the month. Thus the beginning of May marked a new phase in the annual round of agricultural life and involved a considerable amount of reorganization on the farm, particularly in relation to cattle.

* The popular confusion occasioned by the adoption of the Gregorian reform of the Julian calendar in the mid-seventeenth century led to a doubling of festivals so that 30 April was known as New May Eve (Oíche Bhealtaine Úr), and 1 May as New May Day (Lá Bhealtaine Úr), while 11 May was known as Old May Eve (Oíche Shean Bhealtaine) and 12 May as Old May Day (Lá Shean Bhealtaine). Cf in this connection MacNeill (1982), 20-24, and MS 1096, 406 (Co. Donegal). These designations for the festival of May were still fresh in the minds of old people in the *Gaeltacht* or Irish-speaking areas of Ireland in the 1940s. In parts of Co. Donegal 'between the two Mays' is mentioned as a period of time during which certain farm activities should be completed, such as transferring stock to the mountain pastures (MS 1096, 413 – The Rosses, 440 – Cloghaneely), sowing potatoes (MS 1096, 414 – The Rosses, 477 – Tamney, Letterkenny), manuring meadowland with seaweed (MS 1096, 476 – Tamney), or turf-cutting(MS 1096, 414 – The Rosses).

Patricia Lysaght

Cattle, especially milch cows, have played a vital role in the Irish economy from ancient times, and milk and its products have been a mainstay in the diet, probably from the prehistoric period (Lucas 1960). Early and medieval Irish literature, both sacred and secular, reflects the paramount importance of milk in the diet. Lay and military English observers of Irish affairs from the sixteenth century report that the ordinary people lived almost entirely on milk and its products during the summer season. 'The diet of the people is Milk, sweet and sower, thick and thin, which also is their drink in Summertime,' wrote Sir William Petty towards the end of the seventeenth century (Lucas 1960: 21). In later times butter remained not only a primary food item but was also a major source of revenue, and among the commercial centres involved in the butter industry in the nineteenth century, the Cork butter market – once the largest in the world and servicing the huge butter output of the rich dairying areas of the southwest – had pre-eminent position (Donnelly 1971: 160-63; Kennedy 1906: 175-7). Despite changes in diet, especially with the adoption of the potato (Lysaght 1986: 85-7) and tea (Lysaght 1987) as the common food and beverage of all social classes by the late nineteenth century, milk and milk products remain a mainstay of Irish diet to the present time.

In mythological terms too the beginning of May was a time of crucial significance for the farmer. With milk and dairy produce so prominent in the diet and economy, it was vital that the short dairying season should be as productive and successful as possible. Any fluctuations in milk and butter yields in the course of the season were feared and abhorred. The real reasons for declining yields were but imperfectly understood and were widely attributed to the intervention of evilly disposed persons who, through a variety of magical means, were believed to have stolen the 'profit' of the farmer's herd on May Eve or May Day.

The duration of May Eve and May Day was traditionally regarded as a period of time during which one's luck for the coming year, particularly in relation to dairy produce, was in the balance (Danaher 1972: 109 ff.). Commenting on the ambivalent nature of the interface between two contrasting periods of time, Proinsias MacCana remarks,

> It is well known that numerous peoples throughout the world have attached a very special significance to the juncture or interstice between two distinct temporal periods, regarding it in some sense as a time outside of time or as a temporary resumption of mythic or primordial time. (MacCana 1970: 127)

Certainly, as far as *Bealtaine* is concerned there was traditional recognition that the boundary feastday itself, and more especially the eve of the feast, was charged with a peculiar preternatural energy, which had

Bealtaine: Irish Maytime Customs . . .

a propensity for both good and evil. Between sunset on May Eve and noon on May Day, milk and butter were considered to be especially at risk, and the normal competition between neighbouring dairy producers could, and seemingly often did, reach fever pitch at this time, as the fear of hostile intent and activity in relation to each other's milk and butter supply was fanned by the insecurity and ambivalence of the moment (Danaher 1972: 109-18).

A particularly rich source of information about the large body of belief and custom which surrounds the May festival, especially in relation to milch cows and butter production, is that of the archival records of the Archive of the Department of Irish Folklore, University College, Dublin. These records include replies to a questionnaire on May Day issued by the Irish Folklore Commission in the 1940s,* and these, together with other archival records, both earlier and later,† reveal a wide range of activities, aimed on the one hand at stealing the milk 'profit' and, on the other, at protecting one's own milk and butter supplies from evilly intentioned people. This material also reveals that in the 1940s many people in Ireland still believed that their milk 'profit' could be stolen at Maytime, and that they felt obliged to take measures, sanctioned by tradition, to avert such a possibility. There is also implicit (and sometimes explicit) acknowledgement and acceptance in these records that these measures – occasionally referred to as charms or spells, and more often as *piseóga* (often anglicized to pishogues or pishrogues and meaning superstitious acts) – are magical acts that can achieve desired protective or destructive effects in relation to dairy produce during the May festival, if they are performed in the prescribed manner and within the prescribed period of time.

In this short article it is possible only to outline the variety of activities and modes of performance traditionally regarded either as milk- and butter-stealing acts or as apotropaic measures undertaken to counteract such activities, which the folklore material from the 1940s highlights.

Butter-stealing rites

Even a summary analysis of the types of magical rites performed for the purposes of 'profit' stealing shows a strong element of patterning in relation to the time, place, materials and agents of the rites in question. Traditionally a number of milk-stealing rites could be attempted

---

* These replies are bound in the folklore MSS volumes 1095-1097 in the Archive of the Department of Irish Folklore, University College Dublin, and remain largely unpublished. cf. Lysaght 1991, 76.
† In this connection see the Subject Index *sub Féile na Bealtaine* May Festival, in the Archive of the Department of Irish Folklore. cf. Ó Súilleabháin (1970) 333-9.

throughout the milking season, but the duration of the boundary festival of May was considered the period *par préférence* for their performance. Within this preternaturally charged period sunset and sunrise were considered especially magical moments (Rees 1961: 89; HdA, *Sunnenaufgang, Sunnenuntergang*). Much of the milk-stealing activity peculiar to the festival of May takes place around sunrise on May Day, while the protective measures were mainly initiated on May Eve.

Some rites affecting the wider community, such as the trans-boundary charming away of butter from several houses, or even townlands, could be performed by a charm-setter at a remove, by reciting the charm, *im an deataigh sin ar mo chuid bhainne-se*, 'the butter of that smoke upon my milk', while observing the smoke rising from the houses and walking backwards into the house at the same time. This is found throughout Ireland. According to collective belief, rites affecting the general community could also be performed at a common boundary point, such as the meeting point of three rivers, farms, townlands, or parishes.

The confluence of three rivers or streams was considered an especially appropriate spot at which to perform butter-stealing rites. One method was to collect the froth saying 'All for myself and nothing for the rest of them', or some such words (MS 1095, 41: Co. Kerry 1947). According to this act of sympathetic magic depending on the law of similarity (Frazer 1957: ch. 3; Mauss 1972: ch. 3, etc.), the gathered froth represented the cream, and hence the butter, of the farmsteads bounded by the rivers. Traditional belief also held that it was sufficient simply to take the water from a stream or river forming a boundary between three townlands, parishes or baronies – *uisce na dtrí teorann* – to achieve the same result. In 1947 a Co. Clare correspondent states: 'A woman was seen recently on May morning at the river water between three parishes. She was supposed to be gathering butter' (MS 1095, 188).

However, most of the milk-stealing rites mentioned in the sources appear to have been directed against individual farmers and were performed after the would-be milk and butter thief physically crossed a neighbouring farm boundary on May morning. What is seldom mentioned but always understood, however, is that for the butter-stealing rites in the pasture to be successful the thief must succeed in crossing back over the boundary wall having performed the rite uninterrupted.

The magical rites performed in pastures often involved gathering dew, since May morning dew, according to traditional belief, represents the cream of the milk, and thus the farmer's milk 'profit', a point commonly mentioned in the traditional records. The object commonly used for collecting dew was the *buarach* or cow spancel:

> My mother told me that her father saw an old woman, Nora na Cásga, walking through his fields in Adrigole, Co. Cork on May morning

pulling the spancel on the dew. He was very vexed. (MS 1095, 274-5, Co. Kerry 1947)

The spancel, commonly used during milking to bind the cows' legs, had an intimate sympathetic association with the luck of the whole herd since, formerly at any rate, it was made of cow hair garnered from that herd. Attempts were thus made to steal the spancel for gathering the dew of the owner's land or in order to 'milk' it symbolically and thereby take the 'profit' of the owner's herd. Hay ropes were also used for these purposes, and a correspondent from the 1940s mentions that a family in his locality with a reputation for such milk-stealing activities on May morning was known locally as 'pull the rope' (MS 1095, 274-5)! Items of the thief's clothing, such as an apron or a sheet, might also be used to gather the neighbour's dew, and the following information, referring to the beginning of the century, from a school teacher in Co. Tipperary, shows the grip which the belief in milk-stealing still had on the people at that time:

> When I came here as a teacher in 1905 there was a good deal of trouble over a woman who was supposed to have a charm and who was accused of going over her neighbours' land on May morning and dragging her bed sheet over the pasture. The R.I.C. [Royal Irish Constabulary] were appealed to for protection, but the sergeant informed me later that, although he was satisfied that the woman did actually try the charm, it had no effect on his neighbours' butter. (MS 1096, 180)

While boundary water and dew were more than usually potent for setting butter charms, well water could also be used for such purposes. Consequently, there is a large body of belief and custom concerning the use of well water in butter-stealing rites. The first water taken from the well at daybreak on May morning, and known, for example, as 'the top of the well', 'the luck of the well', '*barra bua an tobair*' or '*sciath an tobair*', was considered especially powerful for the purposes of butter stealing (Danaher 1972: 133). This is also widely attested in the records. According to the traditional accounts it was skimmed off the top of the well with a cream skimmer at dawn on May morning, while the following formula might be repeated, 'Come, butter, come' or some such powerful charm. The following Co. Cork account of reaction to this belief is fairly typical:

> The people who wished to steal the neighbours' milk or butter were supposed to visit the well first on May morning early and skim the well. In some districts in southwest Cork a row almost took place at the well over the taking of the water. (MS 1095, 182)

If the well in question was a common source of water, and especially if it was used for washing churns, pails or other objects connected with milk and butter production, the butter yield of all the families using the well was believed to be at risk.

The dairy produce of farmers who owned their own source of water could also be at risk from skimming or mock-churning, as the following account from Co. Wexford suggests:

> The skimming of wells on May morning was a very common belief in this area. Farmers' yield of butter would be low – 'The butter is gone,' would be the thrilling cry in the farmstead! Someone would surely be blamed for 'taking' it – always a woman. Yes, she was seen at dawn on May morning skimming the wells in the district. A close eye would be kept on all the movements of that marked woman. Her cows' yield of butter would be strictly watched. How could she have all that butter? She would not get the chance next May morning. The year would be patiently waited for to pass, and on the night of the 30th April, and round into the dawn-break of May, that poor woman's movements would be carefully watched! And woe betide her if she was caught at any of the wells in the early part of May morning, even for an orthodox can of water! James Power, Maudlins, told me a story of a woman blamed for taking Meehan's butter of the Red House. Mr Meehan stayed close to the well – but hidden behind bushes – and waited till dawn of May morn. True enough, on came the woman at the dawn. As she was in the act of stooping to the well, off went a shot over her head from his gun. Away ran the woman as hard as her legs could carry her. Going over to the well he found a wooden plate (skimmer) used in making butter in those far-off days and also a miniature churn. He took both home and burned them and ever after they had their butter intact. (MS 1097, 225-6, 1947)

Once on the farmer's land the charm-setter could also steal the summer flush of milk by plucking fresh, lush grass and pulling young corn while repeating the words 'The top of the grass and the roots of the corn, give me the neighbour's milk night and morn' (Danaher 1972: 111; MS 1095, 163, Co. Cork). The charm-setter might also use the victim's milch cows directly as part of the milk-stealing rite by pulling a rope or thread over the cows' backs in sympathetic imitation of the normal milking procedure, another practice frequently found in the traditional sources.

From our discussion so far a connection between women and milk-stealing practices is evident, and while men were also, to some extent, regarded as potential milk thieves, the overwhelming evidence of tradition is that it was women more than men who engaged in milk-stealing activities. These are usually shown to be neighbouring women, indeed sometimes even relatives. They emerge as mediators of the preternatural energy peculiar to the boundary festival, which they could harness for evil purposes. Some women were considered capable of shape-shifting in order to cross the boundary into their neighbour's land in animal form to steal milk. The animal which is almost invariably mentioned in this connection is the hare, and a Co. Cork correspondent succinctly sums up traditional reaction to the presence of a hare near the milch cows on May morning:

> The hare was a dreaded animal, especially in the bawn or sleeping fold, and it is often told that dogs even failed to apprehend him as he passed away with a full year's profit. (MS 1095, 165)

However, in a legend found throughout Ireland, which substantiates the belief that some women could assume hare-form on May morning in order to steal their neighbour's milk, the milk-stealing hare is invariably partially apprehended and injured, and thus is forced to reassume human shape. The main motifs of the following version of this legend are fairly typical for Ireland.

> This happened long before my time . . . A man went out hunting one May morning with his greyhound. The man saw a hare sucking a cow. The dog gave chase and followed her to a little cabin on the other side of the bog where the hare leaped in through a little hen-hole about the size of my fist. Just as she was escaping the hound snapped and tore her flank. The man followed quickly and burst in the door to get the fine hare as he thought. All he saw was an old woman stark naked trying to stop the flow of blood coming from her thigh. (MS 1097, 72-3, Co. Westmeath*)

The idea that it is essentially women who were involved in the theft of milk and butter through magic is surely connected with the important role which dairy produce had in the household economy, and the fact that it was women who, traditionally, had responsibility for milking, buttermaking, and the care of associated utensils. In a society where fluctuation in milk and milk fat could be attributed to milk stealing, it is not surprising that those most closely associated with dairy produce, namely women, who are everywhere considered to be more inclined to perform magic than men (Mauss 1972: 28), should be considered the culprits. In addition, the extra-categorical status of some women farmers – those who were old, widowed, unmarried, or independent and thus lacking supportive social ties – made them potentially culpable and easy scapegoats (Jenkins 1991: 326-7).

---

* Almqvist (1988: 60) has suggested Migratory Legend Type 20, 3056, *The old woman as a hare*, for this legend in Ireland. For an international perspective on milk-stealing and milk-stealing creatures, see Wall (1977, 1978).

So far we have considered mainly milk-stealing rites performed in pastures after the thief has crossed to and fro over a farm boundary. A further set of milk-stealing rites is concentrated in the vicinity of the farmhouse. They are also performed after the charm-setter has crossed to and fro over the farmyard boundary, and perhaps over the byre or dwelling-house thresholds as well. Once inside the farmyard the charm-setter might by means of sympathetic magic take the milk and butter luck by appropriating dairying objects or utensils belonging to the farm. Similarly, if the dairythief crossed the threshold into the byre and took items connected with the cows, such as cow hairs, mud from the cloven hooves, cow droppings, and especially the cow spancel away from the farmyard, then the farmer's milk, and hence his potential butter supply, was believed to be at risk. Wisps of straw stolen from the byre roof are also mentioned in this connection. If the person intent on stealing the profit crossed the threshold into the house/kitchen and surreptitiously took away some milk, butter or a milk vessel, or did not help with the churning if it was in progress, then the household's butter supply was believed to be in jeopardy. Indeed if a churning failed after a perfectly innocent visitor had left the house, he or she would be suspected of having carried or stolen the butter and might be asked to return to the house and help with the churning. It was strongly believed that a person could also steal a household's butter by taking a live cinder from the house, even in a pipe, across the threshold. A Co. Leitrim account from the 1940s confirms this:

> The story of a man who kindled his pipe when he came into a house where the people were churning is often related. He was leaving, and on crossing the threshold some sparks fell from his pipe, and they turned into lumps of butter. (MS 1096, 148)

While the foregoing rites are linked to both men and women, there is still the implication that it was mainly women who performed them. This perception is highlighted in the following legend illustrating how 'stolen' butter might be recovered, a process which includes the reaffirmation of boundaries by sealing off the doors and windows, the points of entry into the house.

> My father William Keane of Ballinagrenia, often told us that he heard of butter being taken and that big gatherings of milk were churned from time to time without a sign of butter ever coming on the churn. The butter might be taken for years in certain cases.
> On one occasion his grandmother was suffering in this way. No matter what she did, or how she managed the gathering of milk, her churning produced nothing but froth. At last she consulted a wise woman who told her to milk her cows, gather the milk as usual, and

Bealtaine: Irish Maytime Customs . . .

prepare her churning. When ready to begin she was to put the coulter of the plough in the fire and put the plough chains round the churn, then bolt the door and fasten the window, and that the party taking the butter would come to the door crying for admittance. All was done as directed. The churning was started and the irons in the fire got redder and redder when they heard a noise at the door, and pushing and shoving, and by degrees the person began shouting and screaming and begging them to open the door and let her in 'that she was burning to death'. They kept on churning and never heeded. The butter came on and they took it off the buttermilk before they opened the door. Outside screaming and seemingly in terrible pain was an old woman often suspected of taking butter. She confessed that she was the cause of their loss and promised she would not interfere again. (MS 1096, 148, Co. Westmeath 1947)

Protective rites and reaffirmation of boundaries

Faced with a potential threat to dairy produce from such a wide variety of traditionally recognized milk- and butter-stealing practices, it was to be expected that people would take precautions to safeguard their dairy produce at Maytime. Many of these precautionary measures were taken on May Eve, when the festival of May (and hence the potential threat) properly began (Rees 1961: 89-92).

These precautionary measures were sanctioned by tradition, and were intended to frustrate the efforts of the would-be milk thieves. The farmyard gates and byre doors were locked in many areas, and everywhere great care was taken to ensure that nothing belonging to the farmyard, cow byre or dwelling house was lent or appropriated for the duration of the festival of May. As we shall see below, a variety of protective customs involving verdure symbols were also observed in the proximity of the house at this time. People also had recourse to official religion – prayers, Holy Water, especially Easter Water, and the Mass – to provide safeguards, as the following Co. Laois ceremony suggests.

> On the eve of May Day in many districts the father of the house lights a candle and blesses the threshold, the hearth, and the four corners of the house, with Easter Water . . . (Danaher 1972: 133)

This is widely attested in the records. But all these protective measures were rarely considered adequate to maintain the barriers against evil intentions and actions in relation to dairy produce during the festival of May. Additional precautions were felt to be necessary, and people were prepared to use the traditionally sanctioned countermeasures which they called *piseóga*, even though they recognized that they were of an extraordinary and exceptional nature. For example, a

Co. Limerick informant in 1947 stated that 'there were people who wouldn't ever try to harm anyone, but they'd do *piseóga* to protect themselves from the harm they thought their neighbours could do to them' (MS 1095, 308). These actions included protecting boundary water by means of iron (often in the form of nails) and salt. The farm (or communal well) was similarly protected as an alternative to, or in addition to, physically guarding it overnight to prevent unscrupulous skimming at daybreak. It was considered vital that the well water was not taken across the boundary; a Co. Galway informant states: *Bhíodh daoine ag faire ag an tobar agus ní ligfidís d'aon chailleach braon uisce a thabhairt thar teorann* (People watched the well and they did not allow any old woman to take a drop of water across the boundary) (MS 1096, 46).

Magical redefinition and reaffirmation of farm and domestic boundaries was also an integral element of the complex of precautionary measures taken on May Eve or May morning. It is very clear from the traditional material that farmers greatly disliked others – strangers and especially women – crossing the boundary and walking on their land during the festival of May. Farm boundaries were metaphorically redefined in a number of ways at this time. One such way was for a member of the household to walk on the boundary wall on May morning carrying the first water from the well.

> In some places on May morning a woman bringing the water, though she went for it on the usual beaten path, would bring it home by a different route, travelling with it, if possible, on the back of the bounds ditch for part of the way, even though it meant doubling the journey, the idea being, that by walking with the water on the bounds, no neighbour could work any *piseóga* or loss to her cattle or means for the year. (MS 1095, 111, Co. Cork 1947)

A more formal ritual redefining of farm boundaries is reported from some eastern areas, especially in parts of Leinster in the mid-nineteenth century. In the *Transactions of the Kilkenny Archaeological Society* 1849-51, 374-5, Nicholas O'Kearney tells of an elaborate ceremony, which may have already died out in his time:

> Another custom was scrupulously observed after sunset on the eve of Bealtaine. Farmers accompanied by their servants and domestics were accustomed to walk around the boundaries of their farms in a sort of procession, carrying implements of husbandry, seeds of corn, *sgaith* [*recte* sgiath] *an tobair*, and other requisites, especially the sacred herb, *bean mhín* (*recte* beirbhéine, vervain), if any person were fortunate enough to possess a sprig of it. The procession always halted at the most convenient stations facing the four cardinal points, beginning at the east, and went through several ceremonies,

particularly that of digging a sod, breaking it fine, and then sowing seed, after which they sprinkled the glebe with *sgaith an tobair*. They then drove all their cows into one place, and examined their tails, lest a witch or evilly disposed person might there conceal a sprig of the rowan tree, or some other bewitched token. If any suspicious bramble were found attached to a cow's tail, it was immediately taken and burned, and a sprig of vervain, if convenient, or a branch of the rowan substituted instead; for the rowan was potent for good as well as evil, if it were cut before sunrise on Bealtaine morning. The cows were afterwards sprinkled with *sgaith an tobair*, preserved since last May-Day, which ended the ceremony. (Danaher 1972: 116-17)

Simpler methods of redefining boundaries mentioned in the traditional sources include placing twigs of the quicken or rowan tree at the four corners of fields, or sprinkling Easter water along the boundary fence, or at the four corners of the field to safeguard the farm as a whole.

The impression that boundaries are being redefined and reaffirmed at *Bealtaine* is reinforced by the verdure customs peculiar to the festival (Lysaght 1991: 77-82). Four main types of verdure symbols – May flowers, May bough, May bush and the Maypole – are involved in these customs. Three of the customs are essentially domestic ones and are relevant to our discussion here, while the fourth, involving the Maypole, concerns a purely public activity, and will not be considered.

The May flowers are fresh seasonal blooms, nearly always yellow flowers such as marsh marigolds, primroses, cowslips, buttercups and furze blossoms. This verdure type has the widest distribution and is found mainly in mid and north Leinster, Connacht and Ulster (Lysaght 1991: 79, pl. 14). The flowers were usually collected on May Eve. The following description by a Co. Down correspondent in 1947 of the performance of the custom in his local area during his boyhood years, is fairly typical for the other areas of Ireland where the custom is practised:

> I remember as a boy seeing a family of rather elderly farmer sisters go to our boggy land every May Eve and there gathering bunches of May flowers. These they brought home and placed above the doors of the kitchen and outhouses. Special attention was given to the byre where a good supply of the May flowers was scattered on the thatch immediately above the door. (MS 1096, 1279)

The May bough is a small branch or bough of a newly leafed tree and is the verdure type typical for the province of Munster (Lysaght 1991: 77-82). The May bush, usually a whitethorn bush, or just a large branch from such a bush, or occasionally large pieces of gorse, is, together with the May flowers, typical for Leinster and parts of Connacht and Ulster.

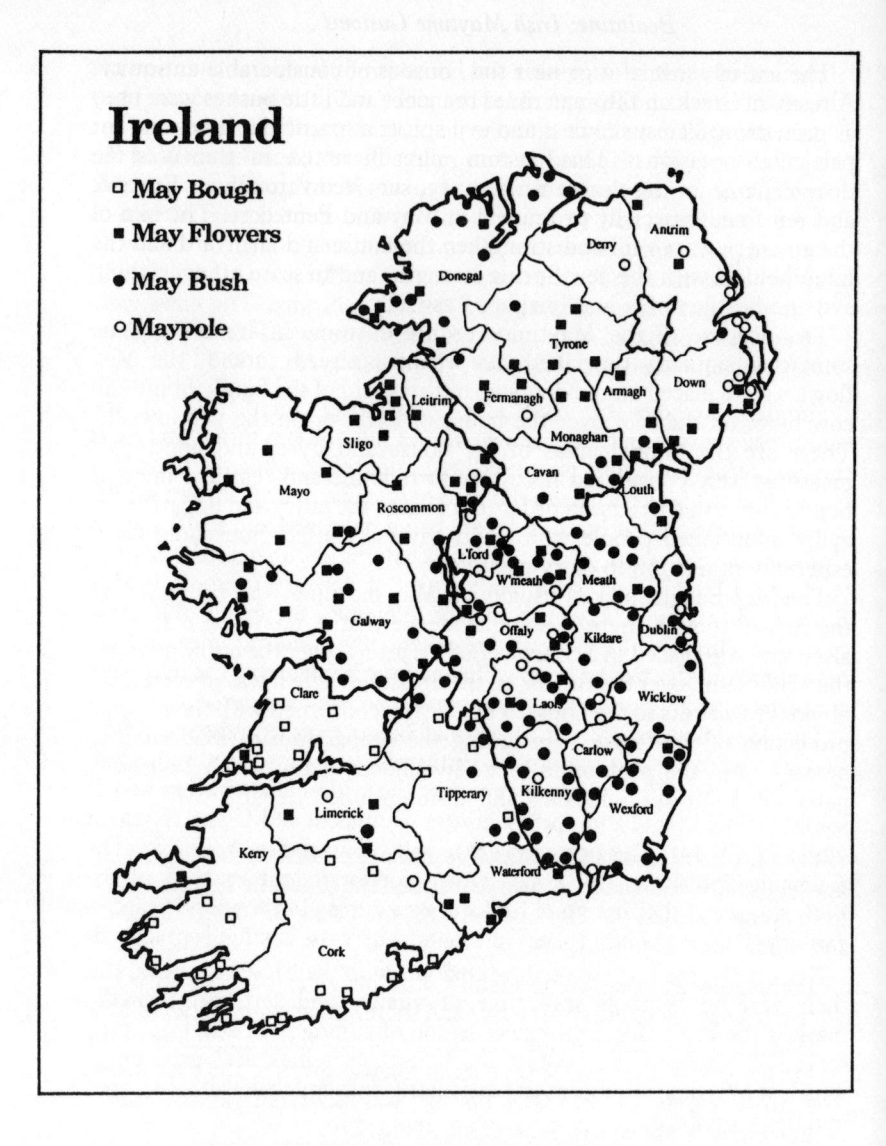

Map after K. Danaher, *Atlas of Ireland*, 1979

The use of verdure at or near the house is of considerable antiquity. Already in Greek and Roman times branches and little bushes were used as protection against sickness and evil spirits at particular times and for particular occasions. This custom, already noted in the West in documents from the thirteenth century, survived throughout Europe, and remained especially prominent at May and Pentecost. The aim of the greenery was to fill and strengthen the house and farmyard and the householders with the new Spring strength, and to scare off everything evil and hostile to life and livelihood as well.

The purpose of the Maytime verdure customs in Ireland can be somewhat similarly described. As we have already noted, the May flowers were placed on the doorstep or threshold of the family home and cow byre, on the roof over the house or byre, or on the windowsills. These are the liminal areas of the house and byre, and apotropaic measures were considered necessary to redefine and reaffirm them as boundaries and barriers, in order to frustrate the entry and departure of evilly intentioned people who could adversely affect household luck, especially in relation to dairy produce.*

The May bough, picked usually on May morning, was brought into the house (though there is some evidence that it was used externally also), and was placed in a conspicuous location – over the entry door, on the windowsill, over the fire, or on the dresser, where it was immediately obvious to visitors to the house. Very clearly concerned with the internal protection of the house – including the preparation of food such as butter – and the promotion of its livelihood, it too was a barrier to perceived injurious intrusion and ill-intentioned departure from the house.

The May bush, erected on May Eve and placed before the door of the house, usually near the gate, also reaffirmed the domestic boundary and in so doing guarded the *Hof* or farmyard, including the dwelling house and other domestic buildings.

Essentially, then, these verdure customs with their festive aspects and their verdure symbols indicative of vitality and fertility, formally marked the beginning of the new season of summer. In addition, they served to promote and protect the household's luck and prosperity, which at Maytime is concerned particularly with milch cows, pasturage, and dairy produce.

Many of the precautionary and protective measures concerning dairy produce at Maytime which we have discussed here were part of the normal 'carefulness' exercised by farmers to secure and protect their

---

* For a discussion of the magical power connected with boundaries and the magical force associated with liminal areas of all kinds, especially about the house, see Hand (1983). cf. *Grenze, Schelle* in *Handwörterbuch.*

milk and butter supply in the course of the year. At Maytime, however, there was intensification of these measures; there was simultaneous performance of many of them in contiguous, or at least interlinked, locations over a very restricted period of time. In addition, extra time, care and attention were devoted to their performance. Indeed, the impression we get from the sources of attitudes and world view at Maytime, is one of very conscious ritual niggardliness and guarding of property in marked contrast to the free giving to the living and the dead, and the liberties taken with other people's property and belongings at Hallowe'en, as the Rees brothers have so succinctly pointed out (Rees 1961: 92); families are inner-oriented, neighbourliness is put aside, neighbours are regarded as strangers and 'unauthorized persons', and metaphorical boundary signs flash – 'Keep out'.

The Maytime verdure customs reinforce this impression of exclusiveness. Strategically placed at the main entry and exit points of the farmyard, farm buildings and the dwelling house, and at the main approach to the well, they redefine and reaffirm domestic boundaries and guard thresholds, and thus reinforce barriers to the surreptitious entry or exit of supernatural beings or evilly disposed humans. They were in effect an additional response to the perceived threat to dairy produce and household luck at this time. By reaffirming farm and domestic boundaries they served to control that threat which they felt emanated from neighbours, any of whom could have the disposition, and power, to harness the preternatural energy of the dangerous transition period of the boundary festival of May, when the supernatural was felt to intrude through the surface of existence.

REFERENCES

Almqvist, B. 1988: *Crossing the Border*. Dublin.
Buchanan, R. 1962: 'Calendar Customs', *Ulster Folklife* 8, 24-30.
Danaher, K. 1972: *The Year in Ireland*. Cork/Dublin.
Donnelly Jr., J.S. 1971: 'Cork Market: its role in the Nineteenth Century Irish Butter Trade', *Studia Hibernica* 11, 160-3.
Evans, E.E. 1957: *Irish Folk Ways*. London.
Frazer, J.G. 1957: *The Golden Bough* (abridged ed.). London.
Hand, W.D. 1983: 'Boundaries, Portals, and Other Magical Spots in Folklore', Katharine Briggs Lecture No.2. Folklore Society. London.
HdA: *Handwörterbuch der deutschen Aberglauben*.
Jenkins, R.P. 1991: 'Witches and Fairies: Supernatural Aggression and Deviance', *The Good People. New Fairylore Essays*, P. Narváez ed. London/New York.
Joyce, P.W. 1903: *A Social History of Ancient Ireland*. Dublin.
Kennedy, L. 1906: 'The Decline of the Cork Butter Market', *Studia Hibernica* 16, 175-7.

Lucas, A.T. 1960: 'Irish Food before the Potato', *Gwerin* 1, 19-30.
Lysaght, P. 1986: 'Continuity and Change in Irish Diet', *Food in Change*, A. Fenton, E. Kishban ed., 85-87. Edinburgh.
Lysaght, P. 1987: 'Innovation in Food – The Case of Tea in Ireland', *Ulster Folklife* 23, 44-71.
Lysaght, P. 1991: 'Maytime Verdure Customs and their distribution in Ireland', *International Folklore Review* 75. London.
MacCana, P. 1970: *Celtic Mythology*. London.
MacNeill, M. 1982 (Oxford 1962): *The Festival of Lughnasa*. Dublin.
Mauss, M. 1972: *General Theory of Magic* (trans. R. Brain). London.
Meyer, K. 1894: *Hibernica Minora*. Oxford.
Ó Danachair, C. 1959: 'The Quarter Days in Irish Tradition', *Arv* 15, 44-55. Uppsala.
Ó Súilleabháin, S. 1970 (Dublin 1942): *A Handbook of Irish Folklore*. Detroit.
Rees, A. & B. 1961: *Celtic Heritage*. London.
Wall, J. 1977, 1978: *Tjuvmjölkande väsen*, 1-2, Studia Ethnologica Upsaliensia III, 5, Uppsala.

Megalithic Movement:
A Study of Thresholds in Time

SAMUEL PYEATT MENEFEE

> He sat down on the cairn by the covered cist ... He looked back at the monolith – and held its stare. Remarkable the power of a stone – for how many civilisations over what immense periods of time! ... And all at once he heard Sheena ask her granny if the Stone walked about at night. Looking at the monolith again he saw that it was not the stone that walked but the spirit which was locked up in it. The spirit left the Stone and strode over the moors, through many places, past silent houses, came back and was locked up once more and inscrutably ... Because this was an 'impossible' notion and had they in time changed it to a urisk that lived in the cairn?

The drunken musings of Neil Gunn's archaeologist, Simon Grant, in *The Silver Bough* open a door to the past and place us on the threshold, or at least one threshold, of a discussion of megalithic movement. Traditions of this activity are found throughout Western Europe – in Spain, France, Belgium, England, Scotland, and Ireland.* Depending on the source, the stones are involved in numerous 'fidgets', variously described as moving, shaking, opening or raising up, turning, circling, roaming, curtseying, dancing, bathing, or drinking. More tenuous versions state that the megalith becomes a person, that a bell or clock sounds from within its depths, or that its shadow 'disappears', or reaches water. These actions occur on differing dates: once a century; once every seven years; one, two, three, or more times a year; or daily – depending on the account. Dates mentioned include saints' days, Christmas, New Year, Palm Sunday, Easter, Trinity Sunday, May Day, Midsummer, 13 August, and so on. The stone's movement may take place at noon, midnight, dawn, on the hour, or at some other specific time. Or the time may be less definite. Thus, the Eagle Stone of Bakewell, Derbyshire, turns round when the cock crows (Grinsell 1976: 158), while Avrauchin's *Roche folle* spins three times when the cuckoo first calls and one feels one's purse (Nourry 1934-6: III, 118).

Movement may also take place under certain atmospheric conditions, when the thunder rumbles, or when the stone is subjected to external physical actions. Religiously inclined megaliths expose their treasures when the Palm Sunday procession leaves or enters the church, when the

---

* Detailed references for the various megalithic activities mentioned here and elsewhere in the paper are given in Menefee 1972: 141-244.

Christmas genealogy is read, or when the priest proclaims '*Et homo factus est*' on St John's Eve. The stone's activity may last until the end of the ceremony, the last stroke of a bell or clock measuring the hour, or (going to the other extreme) for a full day or even a full century. Actions may be single or multiplied, often repeated three, seven, nine, or twelve times. Additionally, stories may have other unique details or qualifiers. As is the case with the circling of monuments (Menefee 1985), a single stone may attract several varying traditions. The *Pierre qui tourne* of La Couronne makes three turns every night at midnight, according to a former mayor of that village, but does so every day or when it hears the bells of La Couronne according to other inhabitants. A local proprietor states that it turns on itself at midnight mass, while a more sceptical innkeeper claims the action takes place once a year (Nourry 1934-6: I, 61).

One possible early example of the tradition is the *Pietra Stulla* of Plessé, mentioned in an 1163 Papal Bull of Alexander III (Nourry 1934-6: III, 548). While only the name survives, this is similar to other *Pierres folles* which still retain varied traditions of movement. Other etymological survivals which place us on firmer ground regarding former traditions are the 1447 mention of a *pierre tournante* in a title at St Martin-de-Boscherville (Nourry 1934-6: III, 33), a 1547 *Roque qui tourne* in Guernsey (Crawford 1925: 27), and a 1552 account of the chapter house of Châtel-Censoir noting a *Pierre-qui-Tourne* which, conveniently, was stated to turn at noon in a subsequently recorded legend (Nourry 1934-6: I, 43). In the seventeenth century, we have mention of the *Grès qui va boire* in Aisne (Nourry 1934-6: I, 216-7), while one of the earliest recorded traditions is connected with the Pontivy Menhir in Morbihan; eighteenth-century sources state that the stone left a treasure when it went to bathe and drink in the Blavet during Christmas midnight mass. To remove the hoard, one must be in a state of grace, since the stone crushes anyone in its path on its return (Nourry 1934-6: III, 442). Most recorded versions of megalithic movement are, of course, nineteenth- or early twentieth-century.

Before analysing these traditions, reference should be made to three general theories which have been offered by scholars to explain these stories. They are:

> *The Animistic Theory*, holding that a belief in spirits which inhabited the megaliths was responsible for later legends concerning the stones' movements (Grinsell 1937: 256).
>
> *The Astronomical Theory*, including the ideas that (a) the legends represent traces of a solar cult invoking the solstices (Sébillot 1908: 89); (b) the beliefs were related to the astronomical role of the megaliths, and alluded to courses of the stars (Nourry 1934-6: III, 7);

or (c) the traditions were based on movements of the stones' shadows (Nourry 1934-6: I, 413).

The Conundrum Theory, holding that stories of megalithic movement 'were told by mothers to their young progeny to sharpen their wits' (Grinsell 1937: 71).

When confronted with this labyrinth of tradition – over three hundred distinct accounts, most of which are interrelated and include both branchings and convergences in their pattern of development – a clue must be seized to allow successful threading of the maze. In this case, Time is our ally. The earliest potential example of the tradition of which we are aware, the *Pietra Stulla* of Plessé, is probably a literal rendering to Latin of the French *Pierre folle*. While this means a foolish, silly, mad, or meaningless stone, the sense may originally have been more closely related to the French *folâtre*, which means 'frolicsome' (Menefee 1972: 145, 159 n. 45). Four similarly named stones have legends divided evenly between turning and dancing megaliths. Furthermore, names recorded in 1447, 1547, 1552, and 1553 all suggest a belief that the stones turned at certain times. Drinking stones occur from the seventeenth century, and bathing boulders from at least the eighteenth. In the absence of any factors favouring the survival of one tradition over another, it seems that turning/dancing preceded other forms of movement, and that circling, drinking, and bathing were secondary outgrowths of the tradition.

'Rolling Stones':
A closer look at megalithic activities

Both the distribution of what may be called the 'Turning Archetype' and its frequency (over half the beliefs recorded fall into this category) corroborate the chronological evidence given above. That the Archetype spread westwards and northwards from France, is supported both by the fact that the earliest datable traditions are found in the northwest of that country and by the large number of surviving examples. Many stones are known by the title *Pierre tournante* or *Pierre qui tourne*, indicating the existence of a legend even where none subsequently survived. English examples seem more peripheral, with single megaliths bearing the name Twizzle Stone, Whirl Stone, Stooping Stone, and (perhaps inevitably) Rolling Stone. Nor are megaliths always involved; the Bulmer Stone in Darlington, for example, is the subject of a local ditty noting:

In Darnton towne is a stane,
    And most strange is yt to tell,
That yt turnes nine times round aboute
    When yt hears the clock strike twell.

(Denham 1895: 18)

Megalithic Movement

While isolated examples speak of stones 'circling', both scarcity and range suggest that this movement was derived from turning, and that such variants were local divergences rather than a true sub-type of the belief. Similarly, dancing stones appear to have been a literal spin-off from the main branch of the turning tradition. This movement has a range similar to that of the Archetype, and may have stemmed from turning legends involving multiple rotations, such as *Maes y Felin* near Duffryn, where stones were believed to turn round and curtsey three times on Midsummer Eve (Trevelyan 1909: 126). Since many country dance patterns involve turns, it is difficult to differentiate between a megalith which turns round and round and one which 'dances'.

The preponderance of examples comes from the French departments of Creuse and Charente, which may mean that the dancing version of the belief originated there. (West of Creuse only fragments of the belief remain, as indicated in the appellation of *Pierre qui danse*, although why this should be the case is unclear.) That there was interchange between the dancing and turning forms of the tradition throughout their development is strongly suggested by the parallel sub-types found for each version of the belief. Dancing, however, was a viable tradition in its own right; there is a story told by a ninety-year-old Mendip granny, concerning the Wimblestone at Shipham, Somerset.

> Zebedee Fry were coming home late from the haymaking above Shipham. It were full moon, for they'd worked late to finish, and the crop was late being a hill field, so he had forgot what night 'twas. He thought he saw something big and dark moving in the field where the big stone stood but he was too bone-weary to go chasing any stray bullock. Then something huge and dark in field came rustling all alongside lane hedge, and Zebedee he up and dive into the brimmles in the ditch till it passed right along, and then he ran all a-tiptoe to reach Shipham – when he came to the field-gate he duck two-double and he rush past it. But, for all that, he sees this gurt stone, twelve feet and more, a-dancing to itself in the moonlight over top-end of field. And where it always stood the moon were shining on a heap of gold money. But Zebedee he didn't stop for all that, not until he were safe at the inn at Shipham. They called he all sorts of fool for not getting his hand to the treasure – But nobody seemed anxious to have a try – not after he'd told them how nimble it danced round field. And nobody knows if 'twill dance again in a hundred years. Not till there's a full moon on Midsummer night. (Tongue 1965: 12-13)

The final major group of moving megalith traditions concerns those stones which drink or bathe on certain occasions. The distribution of this belief differs from that of turning/dancing in that, while it is found in several parts of the British Isles, in France it is confined to the west.

The tradition may or may not have derived from the turning/dancing tradition, although there is no question that, again, the beliefs influenced each other in their later stages of development. Distribution of the legends indicates that bathing is derived from an original drinking tradition, perhaps because it is hard to picture stones imbibing without mouths! Sub-types involving drinking and bathing parallel those of the turning and dancing sub-groups.

While most versions of the tradition are fragmentary, giving only the time of action and perhaps the body of water involved, there are one or two exceptions. R.M. Fergusson, in *Rambles in the Far North*, for example, tells two stories connected with the New Year antics of the Quoybunie standing stone, on Mainland in the Orkneys:

> In the parish of Birsay . . . the legend runs that every Hogmanay night as the clock strikes the hour of twelve, this stone begins to walk or move towards Birsay Loch. When the edge of the loch is reached it quietly dips its head into the rippling waters. Then, to remain firm and immovable until the next twelve months pass away, it as silently returns to its post. It was never considered safe for any one to remain out of doors at midnight, and watch its movements upon Hogmanay. Many stories are current of curious persons who dared to watch the stone's proceedings, and who the next morning were found lying corpses by its side. The latest story of the kind is that of a young gentleman from Glasgow, who formed the resolution to remain up all night, and find out for himself the truth or falsehood about the wonderful stone. One Hogmanay . . . the daring youth began his watch. As time wore on and the dread hour of midnight approached, he began to feel some little terror in his heart, and an eerie feeling crept slowly over his limbs. At midnight he discovered that, in his pacing to and fro, he had come between the stone and the loch, and as he looked towards the former he fancied that he saw it move. From that moment he lost all consciousness, and his friends found him in the grey dawn lying in a faint. By degrees he came to himself, but he could not satisfy enquirers whether the stone really had moved and knocked him down on its way, or whether his imagination had conjured up the assault.

> There is another tale, of a more tragic nature, related of this walking stone. One stormy December day a vessel was shipwrecked upon the shore of Birsay, and all hands save one were lost. The rescued sailor happened to find refuge in a cottage close by this stone; and hearing the story of its yearly march, he resolved to see for himself all that human eyes might be able to discover. In spite of all remonstrances, he sallied forth on the last night of the old year; and, to make assurance doubly sure, he seated himself on the very pinnacle

of the stone. There he waited the events of the night. What these were no mortal man can tell; for the first morning of the new year dawned upon the corpse of the gallant sailor lad, and local report has it that the walking stone rolled over him as it proceeded to the loch. (Banks 1946: 42-3; Black 1903: 3-4)

'Time is, ... Time was, ... Time is past':
The astronomical theory in a chronological context

Evaluation of the astronomical theory of megalithic movement must be made within the context of the times at which the stones' activities occur. It will be recalled that this theory held that the traditions were traces of a solar cult involving the solstices, that the beliefs alluded to the courses of the stars, or that stories were based on movements of the stones' shadows. How do these ideas jibe with the beliefs themselves?

As has been shown, the times of megalithic movement may be divided into four general periods: daily, annually, every century, and sporadically (upon the occurrence of some external event). While it is difficult to prove any sequence of development within these groups, some hypotheses may be advanced which help to bring order to the large number of variants.

Daily megalithic movements may occur at night (specifically at midnight, when a bell or clock sounds), at noon, or at cockcrow. The distribution pattern of nocturnal beliefs plus their general form, renders it probable that this might be the earliest version of the story. It seems logical to accept L.V. Grinsell's argument that midnight versions predate those involving the striking of a clock or bell (Grinsell 1937: 255). Similarly, it can be argued that clock and bell versions are older than noon occurrences. This follows from the fact that noon events are much more infrequent than are midnight actions. Furthermore, a clock would normally strike at noon as well as at midnight, indicating a possible pattern of derivation. Cockcrow traditions, which are particularly prevalent in the British Isles, may have developed independently from midnight versions, midnight being considered by some to be the first cockcrow. All this not only shows a possible course of development for variants of the daily tradition, but also throws doubt on both the solar and shadow hypotheses. It is difficult to explain why a belief featuring the sun (or shadows cast by the same) would be associated more frequently with the night (Menefee 1972: 160 n. 51).

The developmental schema used above also proves apposite in explaining annual forms of the belief. The Christmas night version of the turning belief, found in northwest France, appears to be the only one of our four temporal sub-categories to have numerous examples of the stones revolving, supporting its priority in time. Spreading south and east, the legend could have evolved into a Christmas midnight tradition, finally losing its vitality in a few isolated Christmas bell variants. Indeed, Christmas is the dominant holiday in annual versions, although other holidays are utilized in the British Isles. This suggests major Christianization of the tradition in France, or perhaps more plausibly, that the tradition originated there in association with Christmas and then spread to Ireland (where we find May occurrences), to Scotland (Hogmanay and May), and to England and Wales (where still other dates are featured). Again, while it can be conceded that a large number of versions fall close to (although not on) the winter solstice, there is surprisingly little association of megalithic movement with Midsummer. (It should be noted that 'combined' versions, in which the stones perform on more than one occasion, are infrequent, and that the dates chosen vary widely when they do occur, indicating a modern origin for these hybrids.) This again calls into question the association of the belief with purported astronomical movements.

Stories holding that the stones turn once a century are generally confined to northern and eastern France. This, plus variants that the stones slowly revolve over a hundred-year period, points to a rationalization of pre-existing beliefs. Sporadic actions – including motion at the time of the first cuckoo or when certain atmospheric conditions prevail – are more interesting, if secondary, variants. It may be fairly said, however, that the chronological context of the beliefs militates against the astronomical theory.

'Double Stumbles': *The animistic and conundrum theories also leave something to be desired*

Proverbial wisdom notes: 'He that stumbles twice over one stone deserves to break his shins' (Wilson 1970: 783). Yet evaluation of the animistic and conundrum theories shows that both, although useful, leave unanswered questions in explaining megalithic movement.

Mention of movement immediately brings to mind the subject of animism. Surely stones which turn, dance, drink or bathe must be regarded as human when these events occur? Some versions of movement belief, indeed, suggest conflation with traditions of petrification (Menefee 1974; Grinsell 1976: 54-6). Thus, Saint Cornely's curse relaxes at Christmas so that the petrified pagan armies of Carnac can drink (von Cles-Reden 1961: 257). The Nine Maidens of Belstone can dance or stretch their legs at noon, or will come to life when they hear the bells of Belstone church (Williams 1963: 367; Brown 1961: 395; Sharman 1952: 152; Menefee 1974, 36-7). The Rollright Stones of Warwickshire may become men again for a time, and their leader, the King Stone, is free to turn his head when the Witch Elder is bled on

Midsummer Eve (Spence 1948: 139; Taunt 1907: 40). Yet these stories are the exception rather than the rule, and their very uniqueness illustrates their lack of value for a general understanding of movement traditions. While animistic concepts go beyond mere petrification, and may be important for the origins of megalithic movement, they fail to explain the belief as it existed.

Similarly, the conundrum theory is useful in understanding late variants, but fails to satisfy a deeper understanding of the tradition. Mention has been made of turns occurring every century or during a hundred-year period as rationalization of an otherwise suspect tale. The age of disbelief led to many other qualifications of the tradition. One *Pierre qui vive* in Yonne turns only at the sound of the bell from Vou-Marn – a town which never had a church (Nourry 1934-6: I, 133)! French traditions requiring a state of grace to retrieve a megalith's treasure ensure that seekers will never qualify, as they must be absent from church at the time of divine service. Stones in Berkshire (Grinsell 1976: 105), Gloucestershire (Dexter: 6), Herefordshire (Grinsell 1976: 153), even the Westbury White Horse (Menefee 1972: 154, 161 n. 92), perform actions when they 'hear' the clock strike or the bell ring – 'Of course it don't never hear it', added one of the locals (Menefee 1972: 154, 161 n. 93). Children who watch for movement of the carving and the roof-tile figures of Cornwall and Devon are always told that they have 'just missed it' by turning aside their heads (Spooner 1953: 487). Such glosses demonstrate that megalithic movement had been considered a joke in some cases – fit only to fool children. Still the conundrum theory fails to explain why the great majority of such tales were soberly related as fact. Recourse to this may explain the belief's recent evolution, but again it begs the real question.

On the threshold of an explanation

And what is that question? Not 'Why do stones move?' (animism), nor 'Why do people *now* say that stones move?' (conundrum), but 'Why do these movements occur at a particular time?' Ironically, the astronomical theory, although providing no solution, posed the right question. The boulder near Tórshavn, in the Faroes, which turns when it hears the cock on Nólsoy crow (Williamson 1970: 248), the Devil's Quoits of Pembrokeshire, which meet at Sais Ford to dance the hay (Trevelyan 1909: 127), and the thirsty menhirs of Carnac (L'Amy 1927: 19; Nourry 1934-6: III, 459-60), all break the laws of their ordinary sedentary state at times when the natural and supernatural meet. It is therefore not the stones' activity which should engage our attention, but rather the supernatural threshold in time which allows it to occur.

Returning to the subject of sporadic megalithic movement, it may be recalled that some traditions hold that stones turn 'when the cuckoo first sings and one feels one's purse'. The time of this call is obviously the first day of spring (which the cuckoo's appearance announces), and the idea of feeling one's purse is related to the belief that what one does at this time, one will continue to do for the rest of the year (and what better than to be counting money!). As Lancashire locals put it, "Eer thee ... yon's cuckoo. Turn thi brass over!' (Marsden 1932: 254). It is hardly surprising that stones could be released from their moorings at such a magical time, particularly since the widespread connection of the cuckoo's call with divination (both as to future spouse and remaining years of life) suggests that this was an occasion on which the real world was believed to interact with the supernatural. Those megaliths cavorting when the thunder rumbled timed their antics to coincide with an event which could affect the lives of mortal men and which saw the powers of another world loosed on our own.

The predilection of stones to move on Christmas night is paralleled by other supernatural occurrences – it is a time when plants flower out of season, bees sing in the hive, cattle or horses stand or kneel, and animals can talk. On this and other holidays, water becomes wine (which could well explain the stones' trip to the river), while a Hebridean belief that rocks become cheese on one holy day should make mere megalithic movement a nine-day wonder (Menefee 1972: 144, 159 n. 31).

Two widespread additions, which often occur in tandem (the danger of visiting a moving megalith and the presence of treasure), may also be better understood in light of a threshold interpretation. As in the tradition of visits to fairy knowes, there are attractions in the parallel supernatural world, balanced by sanctions for those who cross its threshold. These may take the form of imprisonment for a year (in the case of some seeking treasure from French turning stones) (Nourry 1934-6: I, 246), or as has been seen, of death for overly curious visitants. While such qualification of traditions is common in European folklore (he who sees the sun dance may be blinded, or he who hears the animals talk on Christmas night may die), it places megalithic movement in context. The stones' activities thus appear not as aberrations but, more understandably, as one of many thresholds in the labyrinth of belief.

REFERENCES

Banks, M.M. 1946: *British Calendar Customs*. London.
Black, G.F. 1903: *County Folklore* III (Printed extracts No. 5, ed. N.W. Thomas: 'Examples of Printed Folk-Lore concerning the Orkney and Shetland Islands'). London.

Megalithic Movement

Brown, T. 1961: 'Post Reformation Folklore in Devon', *Folklore* 72, 388-99. London.
Crawford, O.G.S. 1925: *Long Barrows of the Cotswolds*. Gloucester.
Cles-Reden, S. von 1961: *The Realm of the Great Goddess*. London.
Denham, M.A. 1895: *The Denham Tracts* II. London.
Dexter, T.G.F. n.d.: *The Sacred Stone*. Perranporth, Cornwall.
Grinsell, L.V. 1937: 'Some Aspects of the Folklore of Prehistoric Monuments', *Folklore* 48, 245-59. London.
Grinsell, L.V. 1976: *Folklore of Prehistoric Sites in Britain*. London.
L'Amy, J.H. 1927: *Jersey Folk Lore*. Jersey.
Marsden, F.H. 1932: 'Some Notes on the Folklore of Upper Calderdale', *Folklore* 43, 249-72.
Menefee, S.P. 1972: 'Studies in Megalithic Folklore: a Series of Papers presented to fulfill the Requirements for the Scholar of the House Major', New Haven, CT. Yale University.
Menefee, S.P. 1974: 'The Merry Maidens and the Noce de Pierre', *Folklore* 85, 23-42. London.
Menefee, S.P. 1985: 'Circling as an Entrance to the Otherworld', *Folklore* 96, 3-20. London.
Nourry, E. (P. Saintyves pseud.) 1934-6: *Corpus de folklore prehistorique en France et dans les colonies françaises* (3 vols). Paris.
Sébillot, P-Y. 1908: *Le folklore de la Bretagne* II. Paris.
Sharman, V.D. 1952: *Folk Tales of Devon*. London.
Spence, L. 1948: *The Minor Traditions of British Mythology*. London.
Spooner, B.C. 1953: 'The Stone Circles of Cornwall', *Folklore* 64, 484-7. London.
Taunt, H.W. 1907: *The Rollright Stones: the Stonehenge of Oxford*. Oxford.
Tongue, R.L. 1965: *County Folk-Lore* VIII: *Somerset Folklore*. London.
Trevelyan, M. 1909: *Folk-Lore and Folk-Stories of Wales*. London.
Williams, M. 1963: 'Folklore and Placenames', *Folklore* 74, 361-76. London.
Williamson, K. 1970 (1948): *The Atlantic Islands: a Study of the Faeroe Life and Scene*. London.
Wilson, F.P. 1970 (rev.): *The Oxford Dictionary of English Proverbs*. Oxford.

Another Island Close at Hand: The Irish Immramma and the Travelogue

JULIETTE WOOD

Lured by the unknown and haunted by dreams of what lies beyond the horizon, voyagers have set out to explore and to find adventure. The varied landscapes and inhabitants which have been created for this unknown are not, however, mere whimsy; rather, they reflect cultural attitudes about the spatial organization of the world, prepare men for what to expect in the unknown and, in part, condition their reaction to it. Classical and medieval geographers peopled the remote and not so remote corners of the earth with fantastic races and topography. Religious tradition produced a literature which gave men a glimpse of the rewards and punishments which awaited them beyond the boundaries of earthly life and of the remote and beautiful Earthly Paradise which was a foretaste of the afterlife. Folk tradition and many genres of imaginative literature drew on these sources and contributed their own elements, creating a rich interweave of belief, factual knowledge and expectation. Geographic exploration dispelled some of these notions and created others, but the underlying dichotomy between the familiar and the foreign remained, and travel whether real or imaginary involved crossing the boundary between the two. Expectations about alien lands and peoples are still important factors in situations of culture contact, and whether they are found in the context of geographical, religious or folk literature, they are a means of both classifying and apprehending the foreign.

The current study draws on a wide range of popular and travel material to illustrate the spatial organization of the foreign in a context that can be termed 'medieval', although many of the ideas discussed below precede this time period and some are still current. Evidence is taken from Norse, Irish, Welsh or Italian sources: all cultures whose extensive geographic and folk material present an opportunity to examine the relationships between travel accounts and tales.[*] The intent

---

[*] The material presented here is drawn from a Ph.D. thesis presented to the University of Pennsylvania in 1976. The thesis attempted an examination of the nature of the foreign in medieval cosmology as presented in various types of geographical writing and in folktales and other narratives in which traditional material played a significant role. The present paper is a small section of this study

of this paper is to suggest that geographic and folk material share a common structure – that of a bound familar area surrounded by an unfamiliar one, foreign in the context of travel literature and supernatural in the context of folktales. This bound area functions rather like a camera's eye narrowing and enlarging to encompass whatever field is necessary, so that the relation between the foreign and the familiar and the location of the boundary that separates them are ever-changing. In, for example, the traditions of Noah and his three sons, the political and cultural overtones of the narrative express the European sense of its place in relation to Asia and Africa in which Europe's growing confidence in its own culture is paralleled in the fate of Noah's three sons. Much the same cultural tension underlines the tradition of the Three Kings who developed from vaguely eastern magicians to spectacularly foreign kings representing Europe, Asia and Africa and ranked in that order. The legend of Gog and Magog, the two giants locked out of Europe by Alexander, was especially popular when the threat of Tatar invasion was at its height.

In addition, 'real' geographical references within narratives such as these, in which the perceived relationship of Europe to the rest of the world is clearly discernible, often overlap with the supernatural world of folktales. In the story of Seth and the Oil of Mercy, Noah's son goes to the Earthly Paradise to find a remedy for his sick father. Without the geographic and Biblical allusions to the Earthly Paradise and Noah, the tale often appears as a journey to the edge of the world conducted by a hero (often the third son) for some magic object or remedy.

Herodotus' statement that 'the ends of the earth' contain that which is most 'rare' sums up the Europocentric point of view regarding the remote regions of the world, but it is important to note that distance is not always measurable, and the centre of Europe shifted somewhat depending on which culture was initiating the travel (Baudet 1959). The important factor in determining the location of the foreign or otherworld environment is the location of the boundary – the point at which the familiar ended – and this depended to a great extent on the organization of the earth as it was conceived by cosmology and incorporated into tradition. In the context of 'real' travel and experiences of the foreign travellers such as the missionaries who journeyed to China in the Middle Ages, a sense of bemused wonder in the face of alien experience finds expression. Indeed many of the travellers actually described China or

---

and focuses only on the *immramma*. This genre has been the subject of extensive study and research, and the bibliography is vast, reflecting the range of ideas and intensity of scholarly interest. The present paper does not attempt to deal with questions of origin or textual transmission, and therefore a number of important articles have not been included in the bibliography.

India as another world. Jordanus says of the Middle East, 'Here be many and boundless marvels and in the first India beginneth as it were, another world . . . ' and later he says virtually the same thing about India proper: 'Everything indeed is a marvel in this India. Verily it is quite another world' (Jordanus 1863: 12, 37). Another missionary traveller, Rubruck, was less enchanted with the environment, but he still describes it in almost supernatural terms: *'visum fuit nihi quod unam partam inferni transissimus'* (Yule 1888: 162; Rockhill 1967: 91).

Nor does the location have to be geographically remote for the sense of the alien to be present. Giraldus Cambrensis describes both the marvels and topography of Wales. Giraldus was born in Wales and his affection for a country with which he closely identifies himself is always apparent. Indeed his description of his birthplace, Manorbier, is a wonderful combination of the familiar world of one's childhood home overlaid by rosy remembrance which turns a fortified manor into a *locus amoenus*. On the other hand, Gerald's description of Ireland lacks this sense of familiarity and is often downright unsympathetic. Here, describing marvels and topography in a country geographically and culturally close to Wales, Gerald reacts as a foreigner. Even in his treatise on the Celtic languages, the first of its kind, Gerald failed to perceive the linguistic similarities between Welsh and Irish. So much for pan-Celtic consciousness and a graphic illustration of how the sense of a familiar world and the definition of that which is foreign depend on internalized cultural assumptions and not external experiences.

These introductory references are intended to illustrate that geographic and traditional material can interact at a number of levels. Descriptions of imaginary worlds sometimes resemble situations encountered in reality closely enough for one to be applied to the other. Alternatively elements of real and imaginary experience can be transferred from travelogue to folktale and vice versa. Even when there is no actual transfer of material, geography affects folk narrative in that it shapes and limits the development of the folktale landscape. Medieval folklore and medieval geography are related in much the same way as science fact and science fiction. The fiction is always limited by the fact. However fantastic a place of experience in a folktale, it never contradicts the norms of reality and seems plausible in terms of what is scientifically or, in the context of this study, geographically, real.

At the shores of the Atlantic Ocean, Europeans encountered a feature of topography very different from the landlocked Mediterranean and for which there was little information in classical sources. The Roman attitude towards this *mare tenebrosum* was not conducive to exploration, and although some knowledge of the Atlantic was available, the primary trade and colonization interests of the Greeks lay in the area around the Mediterranean. Recent archaeological research suggests that trade between the Mediterranean civilizations and the Atlantic littoral dates back to Mesolithic times. However, it was later cultures such as the Celts and the Vikings who fully exploited the area, and it is within the context of their geographical and narrative material that one can observe very clearly the complex interplay between real and imaginary cosmology.

The function of geography in providing both a range and limit to tradition is clearly expressed in the Irish *immramma*, accounts of voyages to islands, the conventions of which, almost by definition, are ideally suited to geographical lore. The *immramma* genre was evidently a popular one in Irish narrative tradition. References to seven *immramma* survive in the Irish storyteller lists (Dillon 1969: 124), and there are numerous references to voyages made by saints in secular and religious works. *Immramma* characters visit a series of otherworld islands which are often described in some detail, but are not usually given recognizable names. Unlike the travelogue, the *immramm* gives no description of products or institutions, and a rule of one adventure per island seems to pertain. Only four *immramma* texts survive: *The Voyage of Bran mac Febhail*, *The Voyage of Uí Corra*, *The Voyage of Snédgus and MacRiagla* and *The Voyage of Máel Dúin*. The *Vita Columbae* mentions another voyage by Irish monks which has certain features in common with the *immramma*, and the earliest dated voyage in Irish tradition is probably that of Cormac and his followers who sailed from Ireland in the seventh century (Oscamp 1970: 18). An *immramma*-like tale, the *Navigatio Brendani*, dates from a later period than the other voyages which are mostly eighth- and ninth-century works. Brendan was an historical sixth-century monk, and his pilgrim and missionary visits to Irish monasteries would have involved a great deal of actual sea travel.

Welsh, Cornish and Breton saints go on pilgrimages and peregrinations involving travel by sea. Often the travels are accomplished by magical means and involve marvellous adventures, but Ireland seems to be the only area where there is firm evidence for the *immramma* form. Some Norse sagas contain episodes which may have been influenced by the Irish voyage tradition (Wright 1965: 348) and some incidents in the voyage of Sindbad may be based on, or at least influenced by, *Navigatio Brendani*. The *immramma* material dates from the eighth to the tenth centuries, during the time when Christianity and Greco-Roman culture were replacing the Iron Age institutions of pagan Ireland. One of the results of this change was the increase of literacy and the spread of learning, both Latin and Irish, through the institution of monasteries founded throughout the British Isles and the spread of insular learning, again through monastic culture, to the western areas of continental Europe. Much of the oral pagan tradition was committed to writing during this time; a great deal was Christianized in the process, and some classical influences remained. One of the most stimulating books in the last twenty years on Celtic civilization has been that of the Rees brothers (Rees 1961). Their ideas on the position of the *immramma* within the Celtic background of Irish tradition, while somewhat controversial, have sparked a great deal of further research. A consideration of all the aspects of such a complex form is impossible within the confines of a single paper, and the present study is limited to the geographical aspect of the narratives.

The real and the imagined worlds seem to have become conflated in the *immramma*. Few references to continental Europe exist in the Irish voyages, but it is definitely there, if only as an obstacle to sailing east. The island environment of the voyages reflects the actual geography of the western edge of Europe. In many ways the genre parallels the Odyssey, which also describes a voyage from island to island. Like the *immramma*, it follows the pattern of one adventure per island, and again like the *immramma*, the Odyssey reflects the island-rich Mediterranean.

Exploration and sea travel at this period in Ireland depended on the technology of the curragh. Voyages in the *immramma* are made in these light skin-covered boats which were extremely seaworthy and large enough for men, supplies and livestock. The protagonist of the *Navigatio Brendani* was an historical saint. This historical link has led some scholars to see the tale as a garbled version of actual voyages to places as remote as the West Indies (Ashe 1962: 54, 211). Whether or not curraghs were capable of such extensive sea journeys, it is not surprising that a literature could grow up, by analogy with modern science fiction, based on an extreme estimate of the boats' powers. A more reasonable assumption would be that Brendan's voyage was plausible in terms of the geographical lore and concepts of the tenth century, and the voyages are not garbled accounts of real travels but carefully constructed imaginative tales in which the boundaries of the real world give way.

The *Navigatio Brendani* is by far the most widely known of the Irish voyages. Over one hundred Latin manuscripts are extant, the earliest dating from the eleventh century (Selmer 1959: xxvii). The dating of the other *immramma* has been a matter for scholarly debate. In an article on the *Immramm Brain*, probably dating from the first half of the eighth century, MacCana has pointed out that the manuscripts containing the work come from an area where there was a great interest in native material. This interest may have been a guiding force in the composition of the oral tale of Bran and would also account for some of the changes which occurred when the tale was transposed from oral to written form (MacCana 1972: 102). The *Voyage of Máel Dúin* is one of the longest *immramma* and may be as early as the eighth century, although the existing texts are much later (Oscamp 1970: 18). The hero follows the usual pattern in setting out for a specific purpose (avenging his father's murder) and succeeds after a series of adventures. These voyages came to be seen as penitential, but in both *Máel Dúin* and *Bran* they resemble the testing of a hero as much as a search for salvation.

A number of *immramma* themes seem to translate easily into Christian terms. One instance is the concept of *geis* (a magical prohibition) as when Máel Dúin breaks the *geis* by taking too many companions. Early in the voyage, he sails close to the island harbouring his father's murderers, but a storm arises and he returns only after he loses his extra companion. It is easy to see how such a theme could become fused with the idea of Christian repentance. In the *Voyage of Ui Corra* the penitential aspect is even more clearly emphasized (Stokes 1893: 22 ff.; Dillon 1969: 130). The three brothers were promised to the Devil at birth, but after one has a vision of Hell, they embark on their voyage of salvation. The *Voyage of Snédgus and MacRiagla* is set against the background of an historical uprising. Although the tale exists in a fifteenth-century redaction, it was probably composed earlier (Stokes 1888: 25, 41). The exact reason for the voyage is unclear; the two clerics Snédgus and MacRiagla bring news of banishment to the men of Ross, and then they themselves embark on a journey until they reach the island of an hospitable king who gives them a warning for the people of Ireland.

A striking feature of the *immramma* is that the adventures always occur in a place which, if not specifically designated as an otherworld, is clearly not the ordinary world. Snédgus and MacRiagla's adventures begin when the wind drives them northward into the outer ocean (*n-ocian n-imechtrach*) (Stokes 1888: 41). Brendan and his men ship their oars and allow the sea to carry them (Selmer 1959: 12) and Máel Dúin is blown off course by a storm (Selmer 1959: 40). Given that the Irish were, of necessity, competent navigators, the randomness of the voyaging may be an indication that the characters are sailing out of the known world into an area where the skills of normal experience, such as navigation, have no relevance. The Irish were very much at home in the Atlantic, and an extensive tradition of sea poetry developed which described the Atlantic in all its moods (Murphy 1961: 67, 79). In light of this it is a little surprising to find that the *immramma* sea lacks character. Only the *Navigatio Brendani* notes sailing times between islands, and while monsters attack out of the sea, the water itself seems nothing more than a medium to carry the characters from island to island.

A number of episodes in the *immramma* parallel medieval travellers' tales, although it is impossible to pin down direct lines of influence. The first island to which Máel Dúin and his companions are driven is an island of giant ants. The curragh of Snédgus and MacRiagla visits an island inhabited by men with dog heads and one inhabited by men with the heads of swine. Descriptions of large or rapacious ant colonies were common travellers' tales dating back to classical sources. So too were travellers' tales about animal-headed men, particularly the *cenocephali*.

Races of men with unusual traits, often called *homo monstrosis* or *natural monstrosities*, were usually thought to inhabit the eastern fringes of the world, especially the islands of the Pacific, with which Europe had infrequent contact (Kirkley 1963: 122). Neither the swine-headed race nor the cat-headed men seem to occur in any specific tale. However, the structure of the episode resembles that of travellers' tales: a bizarre race in an island environment. Cats often feature in Celtic folk narrative, usually possessing supernatural powers such as the treasure-guarding cats in *Máel Dúin*, and it is possible that travellers' tales have become fused with other traditional motifs. This may have happened in the episode set on the Island of Women. Although the beauty of the women, their actions and the nature of the island accord with material usually associated with the Celtic otherworld, in their isolation from male society and the fact that their island is remote from the ordinary world, there is a certain resemblance to travellers' tales about the Amazons.

Another type of travel material which may have affected episodes in the *immramma* is the romanticized description of natural phenomena. Volcanoes were the focus of mysterious and supernatural tales often with infernal associations, and it has been suggested that the episode of the Savage Smiths in *Máel Dúin* might have been influenced by navigators' experiences of volcanic eruptions in the North Atlantic (Oscamp 1970: 74). Other episodes which could have been influenced by stories of volcanic activity occur in *Ui Corra* and *Navigatio Brendani* and the account of the island of the fiery swine in *Máel Dúin*. Frozen seas and icebergs were observed by sailors in the polar waters, and it is likely that some of these observations became adapted to the *immramma*. The thirteenth-century *Speculum Regale*, which contains much of the geographic knowledge acquired by the Irish and the Norse, describes the ice-filled seas and icebergs 'which resemble high mountains rising out of the sea' (*King's Mirror* 138-9). Dicuil, who gathered information about the climate and topography of Iceland from clerics who lived there, calls the ice-bound sea of the North the 'congealed sea' (Tierney 1967: Cap 7, 9-11, 41-3). The *Navigatio Brendani* describes the northern sea in almost the same words: *mare esse quasi coagulatum* (Selmer 1959: 39). In addition, the island of sheep in the same voyage tale recalls the wild sheep on the Faeroe Islands also described by Dicuil (Tierney 1967: 44).

Brendan and his monks encounter an iceberg which they describe as a huge crystal column covered by a silver net canopy, a poetic but still recognizable description for an iceberg and its misty cloud cover. The incident also occurs in *Máel Dúin* and *Ui Corra*. Although real experience may have formed a primary basis for this passage, Biblical imagery, particularly passages in Ezekiel and the Apocalypse, could also have given the compiler a powerful set of images in which to cast his experiences, and it is well to remember that anyone responding to geographical and imaginative experience would bring all cultural assumptions to the event. It is rarely, if ever, simply a question of the imaginative borrowing and garbling of the real. The 'real' itself is always and only seen through the eyes of individuals who are already conditioned by the assumptions of their culture. This is particularly so in relation to those episodes which are closely linked to the Celtic otherworld. For example, Máel Dúin and his company visit an island with a magic fountain that gives water, milk, or wine depending on the season. Snédgus and MacRiagla come to a stream whose waters taste like milk and Ui Corra and his men are given water from a clear and, obviously, magical well.

Iceland, and some of the small surrounding islands, contained a number of mineral wells, and the *Speculum Regale* describes an 'ale-spring' whose water has the taste and property of ale (*King's Mirror*: 134). Although reports of mineral springs may have influenced the structuring of these episodes, fountains of this type were common features of the otherworld which is always a beautiful land with buildings of precious substances such as silver or crystal, and frequently inhabited by beautiful women. Plants and fruit grow in abundance; the trees are often filled with coloured singing birds, and the springs and wells give milk, wine, honey or magic water. Among the episodes that incorporate otherworld features are the island of giant birds, the island of magic salmon, trees whose fruit has some special property, the fiery river separating the cattle and swine, the island of four fences, fortresses made of glass or crystal, magic birds, the island of women, magic fountains which give youth, wine, etc., and types of food giving, and the island surrounded by a wall of fire. The parallels are particularly striking since most of these episodes are found in more than one *immramm*.

Traditions associated with the otherworld could conceivably have been affected by travellers' tales. The lines of influence in contexts such as these present a virtually insoluble chicken-and-egg conundrum. The Celtic otherworld tradition is extremely rich and varied, certainly in comparison with the rather gloomy nature of the classical otherworld, and could supply the *immramma* with numerous motifs and concepts such as the wealth of plant and animal imagery, natural wonders like the magic fountain, a history of regular and easy traffic between the two worlds, and a variety of inhabitants to create dramatic situations. This supernatural material might have been reinforced by travellers' tales. For example, the fictional *Travels of Sir John Mandeville* describes a well similar to the fountain in the *Immramm Máel Dúin*. Mandeville's *Travels* would have had little influence in Irish tradition, but the episodes in both show a similarity in attributing unusual properties to natural features in the landscape when they are located in a remote environment.

The *immramma* context is, at least by implication, the otherworld, although the context is an island. The context in Mandeville is supposedly a real island, although the work itself is fictional. A similar situation arises in regard to geographic features described in the *Speculum Regale*, a serious work describing 'genuine' geography, including a lake which turns wood to stone (*King's Mirror*: 104). It also refers to a floating island where all sick things are healed and to one dominated by demonic powers (Meyer 1910: 6). The fact that the otherworld/real in the Irish story, the real but fictional context of the 'travelogue' and the 'genuine' geography of the *Speculum* are all located outside the bound area that is the familiar world creates a kind of identity between them, areas in which ordinary topographical features can become extraordinary.

The direction of influence can, of course, work from the fictional to the real as the *Navigatio Brendani* affected European geographic literature. The island of St Brendan, and the island of Brazil which was associated with it, were incorporated into medieval cartography and geographical science. One of the earliest depictions of St Brendan's paradisal island occurs in the work of the Arab geographer Idrisi who devotes much space to Atlantic islands both real and imaginary. His writings were known to the fifteenth-century Portuguese explorers and may have aided the discovery, or rediscovery, of the Canary Islands (Ashe 1962: 152). Descriptions of St Brendan's island appear in medieval geographic treatises. Honorius Augustodonensis, for example, includes descriptions of the Sargasso sea, the Atlantis legend, and the lost island of St Brendan (Migne: col. 132, cap. xxxv). A Catalan map of 1350 places the 'Illade Brexill' west of Ireland. The assumptions of the cartographers and indeed of the writers of geographic treatises were firmly rooted in the 'real', and the inclusion of imaginary islands with such regularity and over such a long period illustrates how blurred was the distinction between real and imaginary in that nebulous area existing outside the familiar world.

The present study has been limited to a restricted field and has sought to compare the character of the *immramma* islands with actual geographic descriptions of foreign places. Undeniably a conflation of otherworld elements and travellers' tales occurs, as well as some outright borrowing between the two genres, but it seems more fruitful to consider why they become so easily entwined than to attempt to untangle them. Real geographical locations can become identified with the otherworld when there is something exotic, unfamiliar or unusual about them. Similarly the otherworld can become concretized in the course of exploration. Real foreign places and imaginative supernatural worlds are both part of the alien/exotic that exists once the boundary surrounding the familiar has been crossed. One of the differences between the *immramma* and geographical accounts is that the former have a personalized dramatic dimension, a 'plot', which is missing in the latter. The same geographic knowledge available to the Irish was available to the rest of Europe, yet the *immramma* developed in Celtic/Christian Ireland. Questions about the meaning and function of the *immramma* and the relationship between the Christian and pagan elements in them still need to be resolved, and also why there was such a propensity for this kind of literature here.

The present study has concentrated on a very narrow area in which the perceptions of 'real' geography apparently overlap with fictional travel to supernatural places. The origin of any of the episodes in these tales is ultimately a matter of speculation, although the extremes of survival of pagan Celtic lore and the more popular suggestion that the tales represent a garbled version of actual voyages both seem too simplistic. No matter how many adventures are included in these tales and whatever the origin for any particular episode, the basic narrative structure is that of a journey away from the familiar into the foreign and then back to the familiar. Nor is the journey there and back a passive one, the participants are changed in some way, and this separation from the familiar, transformation and return present a kind of narrative correlative for the mechanism underlying a *rite of passage* as suggested by Van Gennep.

Many basic questions still need to be resolved in relation to the *immramma*, particularly in terms of dating the texts and clarifying the mechanisms of transmission. However, in dealing with the relation between the familiar and the foreign within this fascinating genre, the folklorist can at least suggest possibilities for consideration.

REFERENCES

Ashe, G. 1962: *Lands to the West*. London.
Baudet, H. 1959: *Paradise on Earth: Some Thoughts on European Images of the Non-European Man* (trans. E. Wenholt). Yale University Press.
Dillon, M. 1969: *Early Irish Literature*. University of Chicago Press.
Honorius Augustodonensis: *Imagine Mundi*, Migne, *Patrologia Latinae*, vol. 172, col. I 119-46. Paris, 1854.
Jordanus 1863: *Mirabilia Descripta: The Wonders of the East*, ed. Yule. Hakluyt Society Publications, series I, vol. 31. London.
The King's Mirror (Speculum Regale), ed. L. Larson, 1917, Scandinavian Monographs, Scandinavian Society. New York.
Kirkley, B.F. 1963: 'The Ear Sleepers: Some Permutations of a Traveller's Tale', *Journal of American Folklore* 76: 119-30.
MacCana, P. 1972: 'Mongan MacFiachna and Immramm Brain', *Eriu* 23: 102-42.
Meyer, K. 1910: 'Irish Mirabilia in the Norse *Speculum Regale*', *Eriu* 4: 1-16.

Murphy, G. 1961: *Early Irish Lyrics*. Clarendon Press, Oxford.
Oscamp, H.P.A. 1970: *The Voyage of Máel Dúin: A Study in Early Irish Voyage Literature*. Gröningen.
Rees, A. & B. 1961: *Celtic Heritage*. London.
Rockhill, W.W. 1967: *The Journey of William of Rubruck to the Eastern Parts of the World*. Hakluyt Society, series 2, vol. 4, London.
Selmer, C. 1959: *Navigatio Brendani Abbatis*, University of Notre Dame Publications in Medieval Studies. 15. U.S.A.
Stokes, W. 1888: 'Voyage of Snédgus and MacRiagla', *Revue Celtique* 9, Paris. 14-25.
Stokes, W. 1893: 'Voyage of Hui Corra', ibid., 14, 22-63.
Tierney, J.J. ed. 1967: *Dicuil, Liber de Mensura Orbis Terrae*, Scriptores Latini Hiberniae, vol. 6. Institute for Advanced Studies, Dublin.
Wright, J.K. 1925: *The Geographical Lore at the Time of the Crusades*, American Geographical Research Series 15. (Rpr. New York, Dover 1965.)
Yule, H. 1888: *Cathay and the Way Thither*, Hakluyt Society series 2, vol. 36-7. London.

Thresholds in the Old Testament

J.R. PORTER

When I first began thinking about this paper, I envisaged that I might tackle the whole subject of boundaries in the Old Testament, but I soon realized that this would be far too big a topic for a single lecture, so basic is it to the whole outlook of ancient Israel. In the Bible creation is separation, the setting of boundaries between heaven and earth, day and night, land and sea, which, in the words of Psalm 104:9, they 'were not to pass'; the Temple is a place of clearly marked divisions, graded according to their degree of holiness and who may enter them; the purity laws, central to Judaism, are based on a similar concept, unclean creatures being those that transgress in some way the bounds of their own sphere or nature – and so on. So I decided I would just deal with the threshold and even then severely restrict myself. I shall not be concerned, for example, with the idea of the threshold as a transition from life to death, which is the subject of other papers in this collection. The threshold I shall be discussing is – literally – down to earth, simply the strip of wood or of stone forming the bottom of a doorway and crossed on entering a house or room.

There are two closely related passages from the Old Testament that are of particular relevance for this theme. The first is the beginning of chapter 5 of I Samuel. The Ark, which enshrined the very presence of Israel's God, had been captured by the Philistines and taken to their city of Ashdod. Then, we read,

> the Philistines carried the Ark into the temple of Dagon and set it beside the god ... Next morning when they rose, Dagon had fallen face downwards on the ground before the Ark of the Lord, with his head and his two hands lying broken off by the threshold: only the back of Dagon remained of him. This is why from that day the priests of Dagon and all who enter the temple of Ashdod do not set foot upon Dagon's threshold. (I Samuel 5: 2, 4-5)

There are various things to note about this short narrative. It is a little popular folk tale or legend told to mock the piteousness of the god Dagon, and not without a certain coarse humour – only the backside of the statue was left for veneration – although, since deities are involved, it may well have a mythical background, as is often the case with such popular stories, in this instance the myth of the defeat of the personified forces of chaos by the supreme god (Bentzen 1948). But, in what concerns us now, the story functions as an aetiology, that is, a tale told to account for a custom apparently strange or no longer understood, namely the fact of a foreign priesthood and populace avoiding treading on the threshold when they entered their temple.

The custom is the reality – it was still being observed in the writer's own day – but the explanation of it, an event which occurred long ago, is fictitious; the possibly true explanation needs to be considered later. The custom in question is reported as one characteristic of the worship of Dagon among the Philistines but Dagon was only adopted by them after their settlement in Palestine. In fact, Dagon was a Mesopotamian god, whose worship was widespread in the ancient Near East for centuries. It is likely, then, that the custom we are considering was not confined to the cult of Dagon in the Philistine setting but was current elsewhere, as is, indeed, suggested by other evidence, as will be seen.

At the end of this passage from I Samuel, the Septuagint – the early Greek translation of the Old Testament – adds the words 'because leaping they leap over it'. The, to our ears, rather odd repetition of the verb represents a Hebrew idiom that is employed when a speaker gives a report of a particular circumstance, something he himself knows about. The words may or may not be part of the original text, but in any case their purpose is to make clear how worshippers were able to enter the temple when they could not walk on the threshold. These words serve to link the I Samuel story with a passage from the seventh-century BC prophet Zephaniah. In a section denouncing various sins of the inhabitants of Jerusalem at that time, the prophet has God saying: 'I will punish all those that leap over the threshold, which fill their lord's house with violence and deceit' (I, 9). Since in the immediately preceding verse those condemned are 'the royal house and its chief officers', the reference here seems to be not to the temple but to the king's palace (Ben Zvi 1991: 95-102). We are dealing with a piece of court etiquette, and commentators generally refer to a similar practice at the court of the emperor of Persia in the seventeenth century AD (Donner 1970: 53 ff.). Of course the evidence is much later than the time of Zephaniah, but we should observe that the prophet is inveighing against Mesopotamian customs which had been introduced by the Judaean kings of his day, who were obedient vassals of Assyria. Hence it is legitimate to assume that leaping over the palace threshold was a long established ritual at the courts of Babylon and Assyria, again, something well known in the civilizations of the ancient Near East.

The practice of avoiding contact with the threshold is of course very widely attested. In a number of cultures the threshold is the object of an extensive range of taboos which prohibit sitting, working, treading or even disciplining children upon it. The fullest collections of the evidence are to be found in H.C. Trumbull's *The Threshold Covenant*, published in 1896, and still a basic work, and Sir James Frazer's essay 'The

Keepers of the Threshold' in the third volume of his *Folk-lore in the Old Testament* (1919), and I have nothing to add to the material they adduce and survey. But where these authors seem to me to be somewhat inadequate is that they make comparatively little attempt to explain why the threshold had the particular significance that it did, though this is not wholly surprising, since accounts of customs and rites associated with the threshold are rarely accompanied by any explicit reasons for them, not least on the part of those who actually practise them. Trumbull, it is true, developed a theory which, in the fashion of his day, sought to explain the origin of all threshold customs. For him, the threshold was the original place of sacrifice and the shedding of blood, and, as he put it, its 'crossing by blood [was] a form of holy covenanting' – hence the title of his work – 'between the parties engaged in it, and the deity invoked in the ceremony' (Trumbull 1896: 193). Though, as we shall see, there is some truth in this, it does not seem adequate to account for all threshold customs, many of which, like the rite with which we began, do not appear to involve the shedding of blood or the making of a covenant, and Trumbull was led into some very far-fetched speculations which, as Frazer noted, make his theories finally untenable (Frazer 1919: I, n. 2).

What I shall be attempting in what follows is an understanding of the special significance of the threshold in the Old Testament, solely in the context of ancient Israel. This will also involve some consideration of the role of the threshold in the world of the ancient Near East, of which Israel formed part and whose civilizations greatly influenced it – for instance, as we have just seen, the practice of leaping over the threshold is regarded in the Bible either as a strange custom of a foreign people, which required an aetiological explanation, or as a dangerous affectation of foreign manners. In the case of this particular custom, there are various aspects which require some discussion.

On the one hand, we can place it in the general category of what are known as *rites de passage*, rituals which accompany a movement from one sphere to another. For early man, to pass from a potentially dangerous world to the security of his home was a highly significant event, equally so to enter a strange dwelling and come into contact with a different kin group, equally so again to enter a particularly numinous place, such as a temple or a palace. The point of transition is the entrance, the gate, the door or the opening of the tent, of which the threshold forms part, and often in the Old Testament and elsewhere there is no clear distinction drawn between the threshold and the lintel or the doorposts or the door generally: but perhaps the threshold has special significance because it is the spot one's feet must touch in order to get inside.

Movement from one sphere to another is marked by rituals, because it is always a dangerous time: the period of crossing, however brief, represents an intermediate and indeterminate state. At such a time the individual is threatened by mysterious forces, which have to be propitiated or repelled or avoided if the transition is to be safely accomplished. The crossing of any boundary is a hazardous enterprise, which is why bridges and fords are often associated with demons who must be propitiated by various gifts or kept at bay by statues of saints. In the book of Genesis (32: 24-32) we have a vivid instance of this in the story of Wrestling Jacob, for the man with whom Jacob had to struggle all night long is no other than the guardian spirit of the ford in the river Jabbok, which Jacob was seeking to cross.

It is, then, not surprising that in the Old Testament the threshold is sometimes the place of destruction and death. As we have seen, Dagon's head and hands lay cut off on the threshold; the wretched victim of gang rape in the Book of Judges (19:27) was found dead the next morning 'lying at the door with her hands on the threshold', and the prophet Ahijah told the wife of King Jereboam that her son would die 'the moment you set foot in the town', but in fact it was 'as she crossed the threshold of her house' that the child expired (I Kings 14: 12, 17).

All this will no doubt be familiar to many readers, but I quote these passages to make clear the context in which I wish to consider the custom of leaping over the threshold. From what I have said, we might expect the threshold, being a crossing place, to be haunted by demons waiting to attack the man who would enter, and there is at least one passage in the Old Testament suggesting that the belief was known in Israel. In the story of Cain and Abel, God addressed Cain in words the existing text of which may be translated somewhat as follows:

'If you do right you can hold your head high! But if you do not do right, sin is crouching before the door hungry to get you. But you must master it.' (Genesis 4: 7)

This little verse is replete with problems, and I could spend several pages discussing it. But briefly the difficulties arise because it did not originally belong to the Cain and Abel story – it is an independent, quasi-poetical saying – and because its present form represents the working-over of a more ancient text. The clue to what was originally there lies in the Hebrew word translated 'crouching'. It appears to be a participle governed by the word 'sin' but the problem is that 'sin' in Hebrew is feminine, while the participle 'crouching' is masculine. This has led many scholars to take the latter word as a noun, in which case it is the exact equivalent of the Akkadian *rābiṣu*, the name of a well-known Babylonian demon, meaning the Croucher-demon or the watcher, who waits for its prey on the road. The word 'sin' would then be a later addition, from a time when belief in demons had become unacceptable in Israel's religion, to give the passage a moralistic tone, and the translation of the words we are considering would be 'the Croucher-demon is lurking at the door' (Saggs 1962: 485), lying before the threshold to leap on anyone wishing to enter. It is possible, as has been suggested, that the demon here represents the spirit of the dead Abel, seeking vengeance on his murderer, for in the ancient Near East no clear distinction can be drawn between ghosts of the departed and other demons and spirits, and the idea that the house of a man-slayer needs to be protected against the entry of the victim's ghost is a common one (Westermann 1983: 407 ff.).

In any case, we seem to have in this passage the picture of a hostile demon crouching at the threshold to seize those wishing to enter. It may be, then, that the rite of leaping over the threshold was originally leaping over the threshold demon, to avoid stepping on it and so arousing it and giving it the chance to grab the unwary foot.

On the other hand, the house itself needs protection against hostile demonic forces, which may enter through the door and take possession of a dwelling. This well-known concept seems to lie behind Jesus's parable of the unclean spirit which comes out of a man and then, finding no resting place, decides to return to the home it has left and goes off and 'collects seven other spirits more wicked than itself' (in Mesopotamia the evil spirits, the *uttuku*, are arranged in groups of seven) and they all come in and settle there (Matthew 12: 43-5). In the account of the passover festival in the twelfth chapter of the Book of Exodus, one of the main features is the daubing of blood on the doorposts and the lintels of every house, the sight of which causes the Lord to 'pass over' and spare the dwelling when he unleashes his devastating wrath against the Egyptians. This practice is one example of a large variety of apotropaic rituals to drive away evil forces from a dwelling place – we can hardly suppose that the omniscient God would have needed to be shown which were Israelite homes and which were not – and I shall be discussing some of these rituals presently. But in its present form, the twelfth chapter of Exodus contains more than one account of the passover, and one of them presents a somewhat different picture. It reads as follows:

> When the Lord sees the blood on the lintel and the two doorposts, he will pass over that door [not the house, one may observe] and will not let the destroyer enter your house to strike you. (Exodus 12: 23)

Here we have two distinct figures, the Lord, the good deity, and the destroyer, the evil spirit; the Lord passes over the door-opening, across the threshold into the house, and then from within prevents the evil destroyer from entering. It is worth noting too that the Hebrew word commonly rendered as 'to pass over' is of very uncertain meaning, but there is some evidence to suggest that the basic sense is something like 'to stand guard over'; so, in this verse, 'the Lord will stand guard at the door' to keep the evil spirit out.

However this may be, it is certainly the case that in Mesopotamia and elsewhere temple entrances were regularly protected by figures of winged genii. Four-winged lions, bulls, griffins and dragons, familiar to us from Assyrian monuments, were posted on either side of the door or gateway. Equally frequently, the entrance was furnished with two mythical figures, bearing long halberds, called *sheshgallu*, a word which means 'great guardian' (Dhorme 1949: 96). What is interesting is that this was also the title borne by the principal officiant of the main temple of Babylon, who was the guardian of the holy place and who thus had a special responsibility for controlling access to it. From the ritual of the New Year festival, the supreme religious observance in Mesopotamia, we learn that every morning it was the duty of the *sheshgallu* to open the temple gates and to close them again at night.

In view of Israel's belief in only one God and its prohibition of images, we should not expect to hear of such guardian figures in the Old Testament; but there are some interesting analogies. On either side of the entrance to Solomon's temple were two free-standing bronze pillars, each some 26½ feet high and some 17½ feet in circumference, elaborately carved and decorated. Similar twin pillars are known to have stood outside other temples in the Near East, but what is significant about the Israelite example is the names given to the pillars, one being called Jachin and the other Boaz (I Kings 7: 21). Jachin means 'Yahweh – the Lord – will establish' and Boaz means 'in him – or in it – is strength'. These names could certainly suggest that the pillars symbolized the presence of the Lord, so what we may have here is the God of Israel himself taking the place, as it were, of the guardian deities of Mesopotamian religion, protecting the temple from the onset of evil forces, just as he did for the house in one version of the passover story. When, however, we turn from official worship to domestic life, the older customs still linger on in Israel.

There seems little doubt that guardian spirits of the threshold were once known in Israel, to judge from a curious custom enshrined in an ancient law in the Book of Exodus. This lays down that a Hebrew slave must be released after seven years' service, but if he does not want his freedom then 'his master must bring him to God; he is to be brought to the door or the doorpost, and his master will pierce his ear with an awl; the man will then be his slave for life' (Exodus 21, 5-6). What is to be noted is the conjunction of God and the door. The word for God here is not the distinctive name for the God of Israel, but a very general term for any supernatural being, *elohim*, a word plural in form and, in this passage, having the definite article. So we may well translate it as 'the gods' with a little g, that is, the tutelary spirits of the door or threshold (Cazelles 1946: 46 ff.). The parallel version of the law in the Book of Deuteronomy (15: 17) has: 'You shall pierce through his ear into the door', and this could represent a still earlier stage of religion when even spirits are not in question but there is a mysterious sanctity inherent in the door itself. Also there is the practice commanded in the Book of Deuteronomy (6: 9) of attaching a container, holding a parchment on which sacred words are written, to the doorpost and gates. Known as the *m^{e}zūzāh*, a word meaning 'doorpost', this functioned as a kind of protective amulet. Later rabbis still remembered its original function, for they attributed to the *m^{e}zūzāh* a special power of warding off evil spirits. That the distinctively Israelite feature of employing words of Scripture as an apotropaic device is a variant of an older custom is suggested by a verse in the Book of Isaiah, when the prophet is inveighing against a number of foreign idolatrous practices which have infected the inhabitants of Jerusalem, among them the fact that 'Beside door and doorpost you have set up your sign', a cult symbol (Isaiah 57: 8).

Similarly there are Israelite analogies for the *sheshgallu* priest. We find a mention of a group of Jerusalem temple priests, obviously of considerable importance, who had the title 'keeper' or 'guardian of the threshold' (Jeremiah 35: 4), and the Book of Esther (2: 21; 6: 2) refers to two high officials with the same designation at the court of the king of Persia. How the keepers of the threshold actually operated we see from Psalm 24: the Ark of the Lord, the visible manifestation of the deity, is approaching the temple and those carrying it shout for the door to be opened 'that the king of glory may come in'. But the priestly guardians ask 'Who is he, this king of glory?' and they will only open up when they are assured that he is 'the Lord of Hosts' (Psalm 24:9-10), the one whose dwelling the temple really is, and not some other intrusive god or demonic being.

Not only the lintel or posts of a door or gate but more specifically the threshold is the place for apotropaic rites designed to forbid entrance to any evil. Very commonly, amulets, statues of deities, images of demons or animals are buried under the threshold (Donner 1970: 54 ff.). This has the effect of making the threshold holy, and it may provide a further explanation of the custom of leaping over it: for to set foot on holy ground, especially when a deity is present in it, is highly dangerous. When the Lord was about to descend on Mount Sinai, he told Moses:

> You must put barriers round the mountain and say to the people 'Take care not to go up the mountain or even to touch its base'. Anyone who touches the mountain shall be put to death. No hand may touch him; he is to be stoned to death or shot.(Exodus 19: 12-13)

That is, the holiness of the mountain is in itself fatal.

Our knowledge of such threshold customs comes from Mesopotamia and Israel's neighbours in Palestine and not from Israel itself for the reasons already given, but we are justified in considering them in explanation of the rite of threshold leaping since, to make the point again, this is regarded in the Old Testament as a foreign practice. Excavated Mesopotamian temples reveal that almost without exception brick caskets, containing figures of various kinds, were buried under the pavement at the entrance to the temple complex and often at the door of the inner sanctum, the holy of holies, as well. One of the commonest of such figures is the deity Papsukal. He was the messenger of the great gods, and it has been conjectured that his function at the threshold was to warn the deity, who resided in the shrine, of the approach of any marauding demon. But his role was probably more active than this. Elsewhere in threshold deposits there are found the *sheshgallu* figure with its halberd, which we have already mentioned as occurring on temple gateposts, and two little statuettes armed with swords, clubs or daggers: obviously the purpose of these weapons was to repel any intruder. At least one Papsukal figure, from a temple in Babylon, carries a golden rod in its hand, and it is reasonable to surmise that this had some defensive purpose (Koldewey 1914: 227).

Representations of birds, almost certainly doves, have also turned up in threshold deposits, and these too have been interpreted as messengers ready to warn of the approach of danger, since birds were often viewed as messengers in the ancient Near East and the classical world, and indeed in the Bible, as in the Flood story and elsewhere – for example, in Ecclesiastes (10: 20): 'Do not speak ill of the king, even in thought, or of a rich man, even in your bedroom; for a bird of the air might carry the news, a winged messenger might repeat what you have said' (Keel 1977: 94-102). Once again, however, the bird was more than just a messenger. Under the main gate of one Babylonian temple, the regular brick casket contained a terracotta dove, accompanied by a small piece of inscribed pottery. The inscription on this potsherd has been translated as follows: 'May the bird's claw press down the countenance of the foe before the door, and check his breast, may his devastating step be turned away' (Peiser 1911: 291-2). Like many magical texts, this particular one is not easy to interpret and the translation given here can no doubt be questioned in some details, but the general sense is clear: the bird is placed under the threshold to attack any hostile intruder (Koldewey 1914: 227, n. 1).

Figures of this kind, and with this purpose, were not confined to temples. The private house or bedroom might be similarly protected by figures either standing at the doorway or buried under the threshold, and many such figures have been discovered. For example, a Papsukal statuette was found at Babylon under the doorway of a house in the palace compound of King Nabopolassar (Koldewey 1914: 118). The ritual with which such figures were made and set up for the protection of a house has been largely recovered (Gurney 1935). It lasted several days, and I shall only pick out a few points of particular relevance to our present enquiry.

The ritual begins with a list of all possible causes of misfortune for the house, and what we need to note is that all of them are listed as demons, no human agents being mentioned. Then directions are given for the making of both wood and clay figures to protect the home and the elaborate ceremonies for their hallowing are detailed. These figures would have been inscribed with magical formulae, which the text provides, and I quote a few examples (Saggs 1962: 314-16) which refer to clay figures in the form of dogs, and which clearly show what their function was:

> Name of one dog coated with gypsum: 'Don't stop to think, open your mouth!' Name of the second one: 'Don't stop to think, bite!' ...
> Name of one black dog: 'Consume his life!' Name of the other one: 'Loud of bark'.
> Name of one red dog: 'Driver away of the *asakku*-demon'. Name of the other one: 'Catcher of the hostile one'.
> Name of one spotted dog: 'Introducer of the beneficent ones'. Name of the other one: 'Expeller of the malevolent ones'.

Then the crucial entrance points of the dwelling – corners, doorways, roofs and air vents – were purified by smearing them with various substances: we may compare the blood ritual in the passover ceremony. The house was now ready for the statues to shoulder their task of keeping it free from evil defilement in the future, and they were set in their place with the following address by the officiant:

> On account of some evil things which stand and call with malignant purpose in the house of so-and-so, the son of so-and-so ... I have made you stand at the gate, at right and left, to dispel them from the house of so-and-so, the son of so-and-so. Let anything malignant, anything not good, be removed from you a distance of 3600 double-hour journey.

This purification ritual was fully comprehensive and was apparently efficacious for an indefinite period, but it was lengthy, complicated and needed expensive expert supervision. A less affluent householder could avail himself of a cheaper insurance policy, provided that he was prepared to renew it annually and did not require comprehensive cover. What he had to do was this:

> To cut off the foot of evil from a man's house, you shall pound up, bray and mix in mountain honey, the seed of [seven plants are named]. Divide it into three parts, bury it in the threshold of the gate and to the right side and to the left; and illness, headache, insomnia and pestilence shall not approach that man and his house for one year.

It need hardly be pointed out that, in the Mesopotamian world, the diseases mentioned were all thought of as being caused by demonic activity.

When we turn to the Palestinian region, we find similar phenomena, but also two special features which are worthy of note. One is a practice known from the Canaanite and Philistine city of Gezer, which seems to have continued also among the Israelites when that town came under their control. This is the burying under the threshold of a lamp with a bowl below and another inverted above it. What this signified is suggested by a similar custom known from the Mesopotamian city of Nippur, where an inscription accompanying the inverted bowls states that they are 'covers to restrain the accursed spirits and all evil spirits' (Cook 1930: 86). The idea seems to be that the spirits were exorcised by being trapped in the hollow formed by the two bowls and thus rendered harmless: perhaps the lamp served to attract them, like moths to the flame (Gressmann 1921: 20).

Secondly, at Gezer and other cities burials of infants have been discovered under the thresholds of Canaanite dwellings, and these have often been interpreted as foundation sacrifices to placate the evil spirit and so to ensure the welfare of a newly built house. This theory has been much disputed. Not all the corpses discovered are those of children, and burial under houses was, and long remained, a common practice in the Near East, probably with the idea of ensuring that the deceased remained a member of the family group; and it has also been suggested that in being so buried the dead person became a good spirit who protected the dwelling (Cook 1930: 82-5). Nevertheless, there is some evidence that infants and young children were sacrificed on the occasion of the building of a house or gateway. In the open space within the gate of the Canaanite city of Tell-el Fara near the present-day Nablus – that is, at the threshold – the skeletons of two new-born infants were found buried in jars; since these were not associated with other burials in private houses but were isolated, they may well have been special foundation sacrifices (Gray 1964: 60 ff.). And such seems the likeliest explanation of the verse in I Kings 16:34 describing the rebuilding of Jericho during the reign of Ahab by a man called Hiel from Bethel: 'He laid its foundation in Abiram his first-born and set up its gate in his youngest son Segub.' Foundation and gate were, so to speak, enclosed in their very bodies. Even if we translate, as many renderings do, 'at the cost of Abiram and at the cost of Segub', the sense is basically the same.

There are other aspects of the threshold in the Old Testament which merit consideration, but cannot be included here. I hope, however, I have provided some possible explanations of the curious little custom with which I began. You may feel I have wandered rather far afield, but so often, when one looks into what may appear a comparatively insignificant ceremony, all sorts of ramifications open up. After all, investigating the Golden Bough at Nemi eventually led Frazer to write some ten hefty volumes!

REFERENCES

Bentzen, A. 1948: 'The Cultic Use of the Story of the Ark in Samuel', *Journal of Biblical Literature* 67, 37-53. Philadelphia.
Ben Zvi, E. 1991: *A Historical-Critical Study of the Book of Zephaniah*. Berlin.
Cazelles, H. 1946: *Études sur le Code de l'Alliance*. Paris.
Cook, S.A. 1930: *The Religion of Ancient Palestine in the Light of Archaeology*. London.
Dhorme, E. 1949: *Les Religions de Babylonie et d'Assyrie*. Paris.
Donner, H. 1970: 'Die Schwellenhüpfer: Beobachtungen zu Zephanja I, 8f.', *Journal of Semitic Studies* 15, 42-55. Manchester.
Frazer, J.G. 1919: 'The Keepers of the Threshold', *Folk-Lore in the Old Testament* III, 1-18. London.
Gray, J. 1964: *The Canaanites*. London.
Gressman, H. 1921: *Die älteste Geschichtsschreibung und Prophetie Israels* (2nd ed.). Göttingen.
Gurney, O.R. 1935: 'Babylonian prophylactic figures and their ritual', *Annals of Archaeology and Anthropology* 22, 31-96. Liverpool.
Keel, O. 1977: *Vögel als Boten*. Freiburg & Göttingen.
Koldewey, R. 1914: *The Excavations at Babylon*. London.
Peiser, F.E. 1911: 'Zu den Schutzvögeln aus Babylon', *Orientalistische Literaturzeitung* (Leipzig) 14, 291-2. Berlin.
Saggs, H.W.F. 1962: : *The Greatness that was Babylon*. London.
Trumbull, H.C. 1896: *The Threshold Covenant*. Edinburgh.
Westermann, C. 1983: *Genesis 1-11* (3rd ed.). London & Minneapolis.
Wintermute, O. 1976: 'Threshold', *The Interpreter's Dictionary of the Bible* (Supplementary Volume), 905. Nashville.

WIDDECOMBE FAIR

'Tom Pearce, Tom Pearce, lend me your grey mare,
   All along, down along, out along, lee.
For I want for to go to Widdecombe Fair,
   Wi' Bill Brewer, Jan Stewer, Peter Gurney, Peter Davey, Dan'l Whiddon,
     Harry Hawk, old Uncle Tom Cobbley and all,'
      (CHORUS): Old Uncle Tom Cobbley and all.

'And when shall I see again my grey mare?'
   All along, &c.
'By Friday soon, or Saturday noon,
   Wi' Bill Brewer, Jan Stewer, &c.'

Then Friday came, and Saturday noon,
   All along, &c.
But Tom Pearce's old mare hath not trotted home,
   Wi' Bill Brewer, &c.

So Tom Pearce he got up to the top o' the hill
   All along, &c.
And he seed his old mare down a making her will
   Wi' Bill Brewer, &c.

So Tom Pearce's old mare, her took sick and died.
   All along, &c.
And Tom he sat down on a stone, and he cried
   Wi' Bill Brewer, &c.

But this isn't the end o' this shocking affair,
   All along, &c.
Nor, though they be dead, of the horrid career
   Of Bill Brewer, &c.

When the wind whistles cold on the moor of a night
   All along, &c.
Tom Pearce's old mare doth appear, gashly white,
   Wi' Bill Brewer, &c.

And all the long night be heard skirling and groans,
   All along, &c.
From Tom Pearce's old mare in her rattling bones,
   And from Bill Brewer, Jan Stewer, Peter Gurney, Peter Davey, Dan'l
   Whiddon, Harry Hawk, old Uncle Tom Cobbley and all.
     (CHORUS): Old Uncle Tom Cobbley and all.

Tom Pearce's Grey Mare: A Boundary Image

THEO BROWN

The words and music of the Devon song 'Widecombe Fair'*, which was discussed in a previous paper (Brown 1953), were recorded by the Rev. Sabine Baring-Gould and his musical collaborators from a village just north of Dartmoor, and it was published in his famous *Songs of the West* (1891: no. 16). Following this he received from correspondents a further twenty variations, both of words and music, ranging throughout the West Country from Somerset to Cornwall; these are to be found both in his MS Notebooks and in the full list of songs completed about 1900 and presented to the Plymouth Central Library, where they may be found in the Local Studies Department.

The names of the riders vary in every locality. Apart from Tom Cobley, their identity is unknown, although the surnames occur in the area of its collection. It was plainly a song that belonged nowhere but lent itself freely to local adaptation, and this accounted for its popularity at hunt dinners and other convivial occasions. Indeed some of the adaptors, Tom Cobley among them, claimed to have composed the song, but in fact we have no clue as to the date or the author. One woman said she had heard her mother sing it in 1822, which tells us nothing.

Old Uncle Tom Cobley was a real person, a prosperous farmer who owned several farms and house-property around his home village of Spreyton. He kept his own pack of hounds. He never married, and as he grew older was induced to sign a document undertaking to maintain the upkeep of his children, but only, he insisted, if they inherited his red hair! He died in 1794 at one of his farms in Colebrooke and was buried in an unmarked grave at Spreyton.

Oddly, the only name that occurs in every known version of the song is Tom Pearce, but no investigator so far has identified him. It is a very common name in Devon and North Cornwall. It rather looks as though the name of a hated boss or official was used as a nickname for the Devil. Robert Hunt (1908: 391) quoted the text of a Cornish mummers' play in which when the Turkish Knight is slain a new character enters. On seeing the corpse, he exclaims:

---

* Baring-Gould gives 'Widdecombe', as in version quoted, not found elsewhere. The spelling now generally accepted is Widecombe.

Ashes to ashes, dust to dust.
If Tom Pearce won't have him,
Aunt Molly must.

In Old Cornwall 'Aunt' was a term of great respect, so perhaps Aunt Molly was a post-Reformation memory of Our Lady? The identical play together with this problematic passage was recorded in Newcastle many years earlier (Hone 1827: 61).

The popular depiction of seven riders on one horse – unless they were seven dwarfs – is an absurdity not implied in the song: Cobley and his six companions plainly met and continued each on his own mount. And nowhere is the man identified who borrowed the mare in the first place, the 'I' of the song.

For any horse the journey across the moor is a pretty arduous one and far too tough if following the lanes improperly shod. We need to remind ourselves that farming and tin mining were the basic occupations of Dartmoor, and the folklore of these people is associated with the means of livelihood. The mineral rights belonged to the Crown, of course, and were apt to be neglected in peacetime, so that when in times of war armies had to be equipped and paid, skilled workers were in short supply and had to be augmented by experienced miners from Wales, Derbyshire, and even, in Elizabeth I's reign, from the Hartz Mountains in Germany.

Did these continental miners bring stories of multi-legged hobbyhorses into the West Country? Such monsters were known formerly from Eastern Germany down to Silesia and eastwards to Russia, where hobbies were borne by four, six or even eight lads, and it was said of them: 'Le cheval a beaucoup de pieds' (Dumézil 1929: 17 ff.). It may well be that these representations are taken from coffin-bearers, but it has also been suggested that they have been partly inspired by fantasies about the Wild Hunt. Our Grey Mare is no hobbyhorse, however, although they were once fairly common in the West Country around Tavistock (Bray 1836: 327-8) and Tiverton (Hewett 1900: 88-9), where the frame was carried about by two stout lads.

At a superficial level the Grey Mare is a death-bearing horse, and, if so, it is a rather crude and gruesome joke, since it is Death that dies. But Richard Davidson in a personal communication has made a suggestion at a deeper level: the team which 'skirls and groans' at the end of the song are all ghosts who have failed to get to Widecombe because the system has broken down. The mare which transports them, the supernatural guide, has died. Tom Pearce therefore sits down and cries, and the dead are condemned for ever to wander homeless, unable to pass on to the Otherworld, just as in classical and other beliefs ghosts cannot enter the destined world where their ancestors await them until the funeral rites have been performed in due order. In fact the horse is not Death itself, but the means of transport to the Otherworld. Tom Pearce should have been aware of this probable outcome since he lent out his horse improperly shod.

In a Somerset variant collected by William J. Sharpe, called 'Midsummer Fair' (Sharpe 1911: xlix), a new factor about the dead horse is introduced:

> And how did you know it was Tommy's Grey Mare?
> By three new shoes and t'other one bare.

And a version from Baring-Gould (1900) collected from Horrabridge in Devon gives:

> And how did he know it was his grey mare?
> 'Cos one foot was shod, and t'others was bare.

This does remind us of the occasional three-footed hobbyhorses such as the Hooden Horses of Kent, and Tommy the Pony of Symondsbury in Dorset, each being formed by one man leaning on a stick which bears the horse's head. Such lameness usually implies a demoniacal character.

The final verse depicts the mare and her human entourage as ghostly skeletons. This particular image is not common in this part of the country, although Old Crockern, the spirit of Dartmoor, has been alleged to ride a skeletal horse over the clitter on Crockern Tor on a stormy night (Baring-Gould 1899: 195).

The name Widecombe Fair seems a significant if unconscious choice, for the song has nothing whatever to do with the village of that name. Certainly there is a fair held there on the second Tuesday in September. It is a perfectly ordinary moorland fair, despite the traffic bringing hordes of visitors and choking all approaches to the village. The once well-known Dartmoor writer Beatrice Chase donated a Norfolk smock to a local man who first paraded a grey horse (not necessarily a mare) which popularized the fair.

As a name for farms and families, Widecombe, Widdecombe or Withycombe is quite common in Devon and the spellings are many. It usually means Willow Valley, but in the last century a correspondent to *Transactions of the Devonshire Association* (8, 1896: 770), who asked the meaning of the name, was answered by someone quoting a children's riddle:

> Widdicote, Woddicote, over-cote hang;
> Nothing so broad and nothing so lang
> As Widdicote, Woddicote, over-cote hang.

and a later correspondent gave the answer: the Sky.

Indeed Widecombe-in-the-Moor lies in a deep valley very remote from the dwellers in South Devon, especially when it is snowing. Then children were told 'Widecombe folk are plucking their geese – faster, faster, faster.' Similarly children in North Cornwall were told that the Old Sky Woman was plucking the big Sky Goose which lived in the Sky Meadows behind the clouds, a concept which has a very ancient origin.

Baring-Gould (1899: 195) repeated a conversation between two boys:

> I say, Bill, 'ow many cows hev your vaither?
> Mine? Oh, dree an an 'oss. How many 'as yours?
> Mine? Oh my vaither – 'e's in heaven.
> Get out! Mine ha' been there scores o'times.

So it looks as though Widecombe is meaningful simply because it resembles an old dialect word for the Otherworld in the sky, either heaven or maybe a less desirable locality, for there was a tradition discovered in an old manuscript book found in a Dartmoor farmhouse that the Devil visited Widecombe in the course of his rambles, tied his horse to one of the pinnacles of the church tower and dislodged slates from the roof with which he pelted the congregation below (Dymond 1876: 68-9).

There was in fact a famous thunderstorm in 1638, and the church tower was struck by lightning during a Sunday afternoon service. Out of a congregation of about three hundred people, several were killed outright and many injured; this was said long afterwards to be due to the Devil's action, although in two tracts rushed out within a few weeks of the disaster, it was alleged to have been caused by the just wrath of God against the sinful congregation. A vivid account is given by R.D. Blackmore in his novel *Christowell*. Either way, it is hardly surprising that when a South Devon teacher of the last century asked her class 'What do we know of our ghostly enemy?', some bright lad replied 'Please Miss, he lives tü Widecombe'.

There is an extraordinary and elusive recurrence of the mare image in European and British folklore which few scholars have commented on, with the exception of Margaret Dean-Smith (Alford 1978: 62 ff.). Throughout South Wales we have the *Mari Lwyd*, in Kerry the *Lair Bhan*, and on the Isle of Man the *Laare Vane*, all meaning the white or grey mare, and despite the flagrantly male character of our well-known West Country hobbyhorses, the mare is found over much of Europe. The *klibna* and the *kobila* of Moravia and Bohemia are mares (Alford 1978: 136). In parts of Basse-Navarre a white mare is featured in certain November rites according to Rodney Gallup (1930: 195). The *hinnicula* was specially forbidden by early church authorities at Arles; a Russian Tsar in 1648 wrote of the 'diabolical mare', and in the twelfth century Gerald of Wales described (but had not witnessed) a disgusting kingship ritual involving a white mare (1982: 109-10). From what ancient horse-cults these usages derived is still a matter of conjecture. Epona was widely honoured throughout the western Roman Empire, while the Celtic Rhiannon may be derived from a forgotten cult.

That mares were held to be sacred to some extent at the changeover to Christianity seems to be implied in the famous incident in Northumbria in Bede's *Ecclesiastical History* (II, 13), when the pagan high priest Coifi at his conversion asked for a spear and a stallion to profane his temple, because until then he had only been allowed to ride a mare.

Grey mares have a special significance in folklore, for instance, in the common saying 'The grey mare is the better horse'. It is quoted by Samuel Butler in *Hudibras* (II, canto 51, 11, 696 ff.), written during the Commonwealth:

> For all th'Antiquity you smatter
> Is but a Riding, us'd of course,
> When the Grey Mare's the better Horse:
> When o'er the Breeches greedy Women
> Fight to extend their vast dominion.

This virulent passage occurs just before the well-known Skimmington scene, later illustrated by Hogarth. Another account of such a scene, now set in Devonshire, was published early in the last century in *The Tours of the Rev. Dr Syntax* (Coombes 1810: 200), with a lively illustration by Rowlandson. The Doctor was utterly bewildered by the noisy rabble approaching, but was assured that it was a common custom all over the country:

> 'Tis a procession us'd of course
> When the grey mare's the better horse ...
> When she doth wear the breeches;
> The poor fool dare not resist
> The terrors of her threat'ning fist;
> Then, thus your reverence, as you see,
> With frolicsome festivity,
> The jovial neighbours celebrate
> The downfall of a hen-pecked mate.

Dr Syntax himself wears out three grey mares in the course of his travels: the first, the faithful Grizzle, he regarded with some affection; there was a second and then a third called Punch, of whom it was said she had carried her master for the best part of four hundred miles before collapsing.

Yet despite the unconscious fear and enmity towards women, one can also detect a reluctant admiration. One of Baring-Gould's songs, 'The Grey Mare' (no. 51), contributed by Sharpe, gives the story of a greedy young farmer who woos a neighbour's daughter purely to inherit her father's grey mare. Luckily the girl sees through him and has the good sense to send him packing.

Finally there is the matter of the greyness to consider. The ghost and guise most frequently mentioned in German folklore is *der Schimmelreiter*, the Rider on the White Horse. Adjectivally *schimmel* indicates grey or musty-coloured, like mildew; our word 'shimmer' derives from this, and what is suggested is a shimmering light or glow, a subdued, tremulous light. The verb can mean to be shaded or shadowy, to glimmer or glitter, with an older usage 'shine brightly', 'glisten'. This mixture of meanings may explain why we speak of 'Windsor Greys', which are of course snowy white. So the greyness suggests a quality that is neither dark nor fully light, a crepuscular, indeterminate entity hovering between night and day, or between life and death: indeed a boundary figure.

Here perhaps it is worth considering the Mabinogion story of Pwyll, Prince of Dyved. This opens with a hunt, during which Pwyll encounters Arawn, king of Annwn, the Celtic underworld. Arawn is mounted on 'a large light-grey steed' (Lady Charlotte Guest's translation), rendered by Gwyn Jones as 'a big dapple-grey steed'.

Recently Dr Mary Garland of Exeter University drew my attention to a novella, *Der Schimmelreiter* by Theodor Storm, which was published in 1888. In this is included the legend of the *Schimmelreiter*, said to be the ghost of a grey horse and its rider which appears on the Frisian shore whenever a storm threatens the dykes. These principally consist of an ancient dyke and a more recent one, the Hauke-Haien-Deich, constructed in the middle of the eighteenth century by Hauke Haien, a young genius. Of the two, Haien's dyke provided the stronger protection against the sea, but such was the envy and hatred harboured by his old-fashioned rivals that his character was maligned and he was reputed to be in league with the Devil. The grey horse which he always rode while supervising the work was part of his image. In accordance with ancient custom the builders expected him to sacrifice a dog to ensure the security of his dyke, and when he flatly refused to do any such thing, popular opinion damned him even further. After his death the ghostly rider has been seen up to recent times, and it is always a warning of danger (Garland 1987: II, 195).

There may well be links further east. When an Altai shaman proposes to attempt the ascent to heaven, he is careful to select a grey or light-coloured horse to be killed, so that its spirit may precede him (Eliade 1970: 89; 191). And the famous Pazaryk burials in the Altai region included several horses buried with their masters, frozen in the permafrost, with the skins of men and horses amazingly well preserved. The horses were all geldings, and it is thought that mares and stallions were ridden by lesser mortals. The hides are of most colours, but not pale or mottled, and this exception seems so marked that there must have been a reason for it for the people of the Iron Age in Siberia (Rudenko 1970: 56-8).

Tom Pearce's Grey Mare then, for all her apparent local links, may well represent a boundary symbol which was widespread in early times in Europe and beyond. The grey mare remembered in myth and legend was for many a means of travel across the frontier of the Otherworld, so that she became an enduring symbol, still linked here with death, funerals and the realm above the earth.

REFERENCES

Alford, V. 1978: *The Hobby Horse and other Animal Masks* (prepared for publication by Margaret Dean-Smith FSA). London.
Baring-Gould, S. 1891: *Songs of the West* (with H. Fleetwood Sheppard and F.W. Russell) 1890-1922. London.
Baring-Gould, S. 1899: *A Book of the West*, vol.I (Devon).
Baring-Gould, S. 1900: MSS Notebooks, 'Songs and Ballads of the West'. Deposited in Plymouth Central Library, Dept. of Local Studies.
Bray, E. 1836: *Traditions, Legends, Superstitions, and sketches of Devonshire* (3 vols.). Vol. I. London.
Brown, T. 1953: 'Some notes on the Song "Widecombe Fair"', *Devon and Cornwall Notes and Queries* XXV, 163 ff. Exeter.
Coombes, W. 1810: *The Tours of the Rev. Dr Syntax*. London.
Dumézil, G. 1929: *Le problème des centaures*, Annales du Musée Guimet XLI. Paris.
Dymond, R. 1876: *Things Old and New concerning the Parish of Widecombe in the Moor*. Torquay.
Eliade, M. 1970: *Shamanism*. London.
Gallup, R. 1930: *A Book of the Basques*. London.
Garland, H.and M. 1987: *The Oxford Companion to German Literature*, 2 vols. (2nd ed.) Vol. II. Mary Garland, ed. Oxford.
Gerald of Wales. 1982: *The History and Topography of Ireland*, trans. J. O'Meara. Penguin Books. Harmondsworth.
Hewett, S. 1900: *Nummits and Crummits*. London.
Hone, W. 1827: *The Everyday Book*. Vol. II. London.
Hunt, R. 1908: *Popular Romances of the West of England* (3rd ed.). London.
Rudenko, S.I. 1970: *The Frozen Tombs of Siberia*, trans. M.W. Thomson. London.
Sharpe, W.J. 1911: (with C.L. Marson), *Folksongs from Somerset* 1905-11, 2nd series, xlix. London.

Boundaries and the Sin-Eater

KARIN KVIDELAND

A boundary is a line, real or imaginary, between at least two entities. A boundary exists between sacred and profane, there are natural borders like oceans, rivers and mountain ranges, and man-made borders of various kinds. Among the latter are the many separating lines between people, either along class lines or between different groups (we – they; ingroup – outgroup). All these lines create divisions, mark separations and are intended to keep apart that which they divide. Great efforts have been spent to maintain separations on the assumption that without borders no order! Where there is no order, chaos will reign and chaos has always been felt as a threat.

No boundary has ever been strong enough to ensure imposed separations, however. The mere presence of a border proves a challenge. At all times people have been curious to learn what is on the other side and have tested the permeability of demarcations. In crossing borders people have learned that borders are dangerous, crossing can be harmful, even fatal. The danger inherent in a specific border depends on how strictly this dividing line is expected to maintain separation and thereby order.

One series of dividing lines marks phases in human life. Birth, childhood, marriage and death are phases which have been understood as points of intersection of the sacred with the profane and as such are very dangerous border areas which have to be crossed if life is to continue. Rites of passage have been created and are performed to ease transition from one life-stage to the next. The rites can achieve their purpose by erecting new ad hoc boundaries. These divisions result in an intermediate stage where, according to the situation, rites of separation, transition and incorporation are carried out.

The boundary between sacred and profane is thought to be particularly charged with danger. In the Old Testament, II Samuel 6, it is reported how Uzzah is killed by Jahwe because he – unauthorized – took hold of the Ark of God to support it. Man can only cross this border safely under certain conditions, be it that the gods have given permission to do so, or man has performed rituals which secure safe passage. In Christianity, this particular boundary has been conquered by Christ. Death is experienced as the final border man has to cross during his lifetime.

Although the barrier between the living and the dead is strong, it is believed to be not entirely impenetrable. The departed are powerful enough to visit those they have left behind – they walk – and living people are reported to have travelled to the beyond and returned (II Corinthians 12: 2, 3). Further references are found in mythology and folk belief. The walking of the dead, their haunting reappearance frightens the living. It is this fear of what the dead in their uncontrollable power might cause which has brought forth apotropaic rites, protective rites against the dead. The bereaved did what they could to hinder the deceased from returning and at the same time helped them to reach paradise. The best for all those concerned was to assist the departed in their passage from this world to the next. In the case of the dead, safe passage could be achieved by rites of separation from the living and rites of defence against a return of the dead, culminating in a final rite of incorporation in the next world, which would close the border crossed by the deceased.

As far back in time as we possess evidence, the dead have been laid to rest with great care. Archaeologists have found gifts in graves ranging from common household utensils, magic papyri and coins to precious ornaments. The gifts served to satisfy the needs of the deceased and to guarantee his acceptance in his new abode. Another measure of caring for the departed consisted of rituals performed before and after death, and burial customs bear witness to this. After scrupulous observance of the duties towards the departed, it was hoped that they, being so well provided for, would have no reason to disrupt the life of the community they had left.

For centuries the Church was, and still is to a certain degree, the institution in charge of man's spiritual wellbeing. She performs rites of passage when baptizing infants, marrying couples, assisting the dying and burying the dead. Catholics are familiar with the sacrament of extreme unction, and Protestant ministers will hear confession and celebrate the Eucharist prior to the last rites performed in the burial ground. Yet people have created their own rites, in many ways differing from and often in opposition to the ritual administered by the Church. These popular rites do not replace the official ones, they accompany them.

One of these popular rites was the funeral rite of sin-eating, performed by a sin-eater, a man or woman. Through accepting the food and drink provided, he took upon himself the sins of the departed.

The term funeral brings to mind the final boundary in human existence: the boundary between life and death, or perhaps one should say, the boundary between living and dead. Furthermore, at a funeral the boundary between sacred and profane is felt to be sharper than on other occasions. The sin-eater is expected to fend off the dangers connected with the crossing of this border.

Sin-eating as a funeral custom was performed, according to the oldest records, in Wales, Herefordshire and Shropshire in the seventeenth century, the time of the Stuarts. The period is characterized by religious, economic and social unrest which threatened the stability of a pre-industrial society. The great majority of the people lived on the land, in small isolated communities. The community was the centre of existence with regard to both work and leisure, and strangers were viewed with suspicion. There seem to be no records of sin-eating in Ireland (oral communication from Patricia Lysaght). With regard to Scotland, Mary Webb writes in the foreword to her novel *Precious Bane* in 1924:

> In treating of the old subject of sin-eating I am aware that William Sharpe [sic] has forestalled me and has written with consummate art. But sin-eaters were as well known on the Welsh border as in Scotland ...

This refers to William Sharp's story 'The Sin Eater', published in 1895 under the name of Fiona Macleod and set in Iona. James Napier in his account of folklore in Western Scotland (Napier 1879: 60-1) refers to the custom as fairly recent:

> When the corpse was laid out, a plate of salt was placed upon the breast, ostensibly to prevent the body swelling. Many did so in this belief, but its original purpose was to act as a charm against the devil to prevent him from disturbing the body ... But there was an older superstition which gave another explanation for the plate of salt on the breast. There were persons calling themselves *sin eaters* who, when a person died, were sent for to come and eat the sins of the deceased. When they came, their *modus operandi* was to place a plate of salt and a plate of bread on the breast of the corpse, and repeat a series of incantations, after which they ate the contents of the plates, and so relieved the dead person of such sins as would have kept him hovering around his relations, haunting them with his imperfectly purified spirit, to their great annoyance and without satisfaction to himself.

Enid Porter in her *Cambridgeshire Customs and Folklore* gives an account obtained from the storyteller W.H. Barrett of the same custom in the Fens, but this reads more like fiction than recorded fact, and there is no corroboration for the practice in eastern England (Porter 1969: 26).

The two oldest records of sin-eating are given by John Aubrey in *Remaines of Gentilisme and Judaisme*, written in 1686-7. A third record, in a long letter from Mr John Bagford, is said to go back to John Aubrey (Bagford 1774: lxxvi), and refers to the custom of sin-eating in Shropshire. The custom is older than Aubrey's time, and is traceable, with variations, up to the 1850s, maybe even later (Hartland 1920: 571 ff.). Matthew Moggridge in 1852 gave an account to the Cambrian

Boundaries and the Sin-Eater

Archaeological Society at a meeting in Ludlow (Moggridge 1852: 330 ff.).

John Aubrey's first account reads as follows:

> In the County of Hereford was an old Custome at Funeralls to hire [substituted for 'have'] poor people, who were to take upon them all the Sinnes of the party deceased. One of them I remember (he was a long leane, lament[able] poor raskal) lived in a Cottage on Rosse-high-way. The manner was that when the Corps was brought-out of the house and layd on the Biere; a Loafe of bread was brought out, and delivered to the Sinne-eater over the corps, as also a Mazar-bowle of Maple [substituted for 'Gossips bowle'] full of beer, which he was to drink up, and sixpence in money, in consideration whereof he tooke upon him (*ipso facto*) all the Sinnes of the Defunct, and freed him [or her] from Walking after they were dead ... This Custome (though rarely used in our dayes) yet by some people was observed [substituted for 'continued'] even in the strictest time of the Presbyterian government [1649-1660]: as at Dynder, *volens nolens* the Parson of the Parish, the kindred of a woman deceased there, had this ceremonie punctually performed according to her Will. And also the like was donne at the City of Hereford in those times [substituted for 'dayes'], where a Woman kept many years before her death a Mazar-bowle for the Sinne-eater: and the like in other places in this Countie: as also in Brecon, *e.g.* at Llangors, where Mr Gwin was minister about 1640, could not hinder the performing of this ancient custom. In North-Wales, the Sinne-eaters are frequently made use of; but there, in sted of a Bowle of Beere, they have a bowle of Milke. I believe this custome was heretofore used over all Wales. (Aubrey 1972: 179-80)

Mr Bagford's account is as follows:

> Within the memory of our Fathers, in Shropshire, in those villages adjoyning to Wales, when a person dyed there was notice given to an old Sire, (for so they called him), who presently repaired to the place where the deceased lay, and stood before the door of the house, when some of the Family came out and furnished him with a Cricket [low stool], on which he sat down facing the door. Then they gave him a Groat, which he put in his pocket; a Crust of Bread, which he eat; and a full bowle of Ale which he drank off at a draught. After this he got up from the Cricket and pronounced, with a composed gesture, the ease and rest of the Soul departed, for which he would pawn his own Soul. (Bagford 1774: lxxvi)

In these accounts we are confronted with borders. The scenario according to the records collected by Aubrey is set. The drama unfolds with the commencement of separation: the sin-eater is living on the fringes of the community. The poor, old, ugly and lamentable rascal from Rosse Highway and the 'Sire' are called in, and when the dead has been brought out of the house, the sin-eater performs his sin-eating.

All the records agree with regard to the localization. They differ with regard to the person; in Beaumaris no definite person is named: this text speaks rather generally of people on the other side of the corpse. Both the dead and the sin-eater are located in the space of separation, the intermediate stage – outside the house. With the departed brought outside, his exodus from the community of the living has begun. The sin-eater has also arrived in this space of separation. During his performance the sin-eater stands at the meeting point of the borders between sacred and profane, the living and the dead, and between community and strangers.

The separation rite of sin-eating gives relatives and friends of the deceased another opportunity to adjust to the death in their midst, through provision of time and space. It halts the departure of the deceased and the mourners win time, because the performance of the sin-eater disrupts the funeral procession from house to burial place, and space, because sin-eating takes place on the dividing line between public and private, thereby widening this area.

A death did not only affect the closest relatives of the deceased, but in varying degrees also the entire village. Although the departed is still present he no longer belongs to the living. He has assumed another quality from them, he is different. His new and unknown quality is a peril to the living, it threatens to turn order into chaos. The sudden confrontation with the sacred increases the fear of the bereaved. On the level of day-to-day existence, functions the departed fulfilled as farmer, husband, and father, for instance, are suspended. Replacements and compensations must be found. This is in itself a situation which endangers the continuity of communal existence. In addition to this comes the disturbing uncertainty as to whether the departed will go to the 'right place', to Heaven, and the fear he might walk, either because he feels unhappy where he is and needs the help of the living to find rest, or to take revenge on the living.

Apparently the crumbling border between living and dead was more frightening than the one between community and outsider. But also the boundary between sacred and profane is visible in the sin-eater. The sin-eater combines in his person supernatural powers (one indication is the address 'Sire'), the believed capability to remove sins, with the status of an outsider. He is powerful enough to help the community. His supernatural powers, which also can be used against the community, his status as an outcast, and his dealing with corpses make him, according to general folk belief, even more dangerous than other unclean persons.

Boundaries and the Sin-Eater

To handle the threat incorporated in the sin-eater, he remains in the area of separation.

In the area of separation he performs his service for the deceased – and ultimately for the living. How is it done? In Hereford he is offered a loaf of bread and a bowl of beer *over* the corpse and sixpence in money. In North Wales they give him a bowl of milk instead of beer. In Beaumaris, Anglesey, they offer him cake and cheese, a new bowl of beer and another of milk, no money is mentioned. According to Mr Bagford's letter, in Shropshire he waits outside the house. He is given a groat (a small coin, worth four old pence), a crust of bread, and a full bowl of ale. The first and the third references state that the sin-eater eats, drinks and accepts the money, the second reference says only that cake and cheese as well as beer and milk are accepted on the other side of the corpse.

In Hereford and Beaumaris the service of the sin-eater ends with his proclamation that the sins of the dead are now upon himself. By offering bread and drink over the corpse it is assumed that the sins are transferred to them. The sources say nothing about how this transfer is brought about. One might expect that the food had to touch the corpse, but there are instances in folk belief where it is enough to pass something over a person to achieve the desired result. In North Wales nothing is said about eating or drinking, only acceptance of the gifts is stated.

With the ritual of sin-eating one step of the separation ritual is ended. Aubrey's records say no more about the sin-eater. Funeral procedures continue, now performed by the Church. Aubrey states that the Church is aware of sin-eating, and although it does not condone it, apparently the Church cannot prohibit the performance of this custom as at Llangors, where the minister, about 1640, 'could not hinder it' (see page 87 above).

The drama of the sin-eater involves several borders which in varying degrees affect all participants, the community, the departed and the sin-eater. Though borders are erected to maintain order, here some are crossed, and have to be crossed. In the face of ensuing disorder the boundary between sacred and profane is reinforced through the temporary removal of the border between sin-eater and community connected with a doubling of rites ensuring the happy stay of the dead in the area assigned to them. Sin-eating is an additional safety measure within the burial rites, created by folk belief.

The sin-eater is an outsider: he has to be called and he obeys that call. He takes upon himself the sins of others – and goes on living, while Christ himself had to die when he took upon himself the sins of mankind. The initiative lies with the community. Its members are dependent on the sin-eater. To satisfy their needs they remove the border between themselves and the stranger for so long as it takes him to carry out his service. The sources do not say anything about how one becomes a sin-eater, but for someone already belonging to the lowest part of society, it seems there was nothing to lose by accepting such a task. A small amount of money, bread, beer and/or milk would be welcome to a poor person. On the other hand he experienced the power of the community. It could make the sin-eater instrumental to achieve its purpose because as an outcast he did not belong to the human family, and was denied fellowship with others. In this manner it becomes possible for the community to re-establish and fortify boundaries about to collapse. By using the sin-eater as scapegoat (Leviticus 16) order is restored.

REFERENCES

Aubrey, J. 1972: *Remaines of Gentilisme and Judaisme*, in *John Aubrey, Three Prose Works*, J. Buchanan-Brown ed., Centaur Classics. London.

Bagford, J. 1774: 'Letter to the Publisher', printed as preface to John Leland, *De Rebus Britannicis Collectanea* (2nd ed.). London. Reprinted John Brand, *Observations on Popular Antiquities* (revised Sir Henry Ellis) II, 1813. London.

Hartland, S.E. 1920: 'Sin-Eating', *Encyclopaedia of Religion and Ethics* XI, J. Hastings ed. London.

Moggridge, M. 1852: Report given at meeting of the Cambrian Archaeological Association at Ludlow, *Archaeologia Cambrensis* 3 (n.s.). London.

Napier, J. 1879: *Folklore or Superstitious Beliefs in the West of Scotland within this century*. Paisley.

Porter, E. 1969: *Cambridgeshire Customs and Folklore: with Fenland material provided by W.H. Barrett*. London.

Death's Door: Thresholds and Boundaries in British Funeral Customs

RUTH RICHARDSON

Death's door is the ultimate threshold; death itself the Great Divide. The bourn from which no traveller returns is the last boundary: the final, insuperable barrier between this life and the next. So fundamental a frontier is death itself that it is perhaps unsurprising that rituals associated with the disposal of the dead are rich in threshold and boundary imagery.

The first observances recorded on the occurrence of a death were the closing of the corpse's eyes and the opening of a door or window to allow the soul a free escape. Mirrors and other reflective surfaces were covered, apparently to encourage the spirit to find its way to the open threshold rather than become caught in a reflection, which might result in haunting (DDD:27).* Even prior to the process of laying out the body, the face was covered: with a sheet if death took place in bed, or a handkerchief, hat or other convenient cloth. Such simple gestures often marked the first physical boundary between the world of the living and that of the dead.

Probably the most crucial boundary in funerary observances is temporal. Without embalming, the body itself imposes severe constraints on the duration of the interval between death and burial. Bearing this in mind, I propose to look here at both spatial and symbolic boundaries and thresholds, drawing upon a wide examination of folklore sources, documentary and oral testimony concerning their importance in the context of the recorded funerary customs of the British Isles. Such recording has occurred largely since c.1700, but I have argued elsewhere that many of the customs discussed may be older still (DDD:6). Although these customs are spoken of here in the past tense, some are still observed, and many more conserved in memory.

An uneasy attitude towards the dead, a compound of care and fear, has been discerned by anthropologists in the funerary rites of other cultures. Although the breadth of British ghostlore articulates a profound latent

* The references and bibliography to my book, *Death, Dissection and the Destitute* (Penguin 1989), (DDD followed by page reference in the text) are too extensive to repeat here.

dread, our death customs appear remarkably tolerant towards the dead, inclined to solicitude and sentimentality rather than to terror. This apparent tolerance derived not from any lack of fear but from an underlying belief that *due care of the dead* offered some assurance of the soul's future repose as well as providing comfort for the bereaved (DDD:17).

What constituted 'due care' varied locally, regionally and over time. Recorded customs seem to have worked on many levels, often serving more than one need. I have elsewhere observed that many possess a Janus-like ability to be understood either as a friendly gesture of protection towards the body and soul, or as an expression of dread, revealing a desire to prevent haunting (DDD:28). Boundaries and thresholds are remarkably consistent and significant features of these rituals and beliefs – as for example in the omen associated with a door opening by itself, which was believed to presage a death (DDD:13).

A boundary marks the extent of an area in some way: mentally, figuratively on maps, symbolically with sight lines, or physically with marker stones or trees, fences or walls. The boundary protects its enclosure, limits or curtails movement within and without, encourages settlement, containment, states the extent of ownership or affiliation. A threshold breaches a boundary, and implies movement, in or out. Thresholds and boundaries are in some sense interchangeable; a door if locked becomes a boundary, open, a threshold. These important barriers determine routes of access, egress, or circumnavigation.

When after a marriage a bride was lifted by her groom over the threshold, the act marked a boundary between one phase of life and another for both individuals. In entering the house together, the couple passed from the outdoor/public part of the ceremony to their own private world. The symbolism was of a new life together in an enclosure, a relationship, a home. Funerary rites reversed the process, the private world was left behind for an outdoor/public procession and ceremony, and place of disposal. Symbols of joy and togetherness were replaced by those of sorrow and separation. A series of thresholds and boundaries punctuated the journey between home and the 'long home'.

Within hours of death, the washing and preparation of the dead body involved the reinforcement of the physical outline of the body itself (DDD:21). Mouth and eyes were closed and if necessary held shut, the chin with a bandage or chinstrap, the eyes, most commonly, with pennies. Thus the body's natural thresholds were sealed. Other orifices were plugged, and the body given a simple outline by the straightening and securing of limbs: thumbs and big toes were usually tied together, and often knees and ankles too. In earlier times the body was then further enclosed by shrouding in a winding sheet – tied or knotted at head and foot – or dressed and placed in bed or in a coffin for viewing by visitors.

Exposure of the face would be facilitated by means of a small flap or gap left in the winding sheet, or by the use of a facecloth, which would be lifted when a visitor came to make a last farewell. In most cases, the body would be ready in its coffin when visitors were ushered in, the winding sheet parted, the facecloth lifted, or the coffin lid slid back to expose the face. Both the latter procedures are shown in eighteenth-century engravings (DDD:18, 26).

From the time of a death, thresholds in the house of death took on an added importance. When the physical preparation of the dead body was complete, an interval of several days was usually observed before the funeral. An early eighteenth-century observer noted:

> which Time they allow, as well to give the dead Person an opportunity of coming to Life again, if his Soul has not quite left his Body, as to prepare Mourning, and the Ceremonies of the Funeral.
> (Misson 1719: 88-93)

Shutting a door upon a corpse during this important period was considered to invite bad luck or to presage another death, and for the same reasons the body is said not to have been left alone (DDD:12-14, 22).

Windows were shrouded as blinds or curtains were drawn, and doors are said to have had bells and door knockers muffled in black fabric. Among those who could spend considerable amounts of money on funerary pomp, it was also usual to hang a hatchment above or beside the door of the house, showing the family heraldry, or an undertaker's version thereof, suitably displayed to signify the event of death. Mutes – two men bearing wands shrouded in black – were paid to stand at either side of the front door during daylight hours (Puckle 1926: 96; Morley 1971: pl. 19).

In some rural districts, it was customary for the coffin to be stood outside the front door on trestles (Bewick 1962: pl. 163/5; Addy 1895: 124). In times of plague doors were marked 'Lord Have Mercy' by way of warning, and sealed to prevent spread of the disease, often confining the healthy with the sick (Slack 1985: 262, 271). In happier recent times, plaques commemorating an association with a deceased writer or other personage might be erected on the house front, usually near the front door. In some northern towns, and in parts of the East End of London, on the day of the funeral it was customary to place wreaths and flowers by the front door or garden gate so that neighbours could see what had been purchased in their name from local collections of money (Richardson 1978).

As will be clear from these examples, the threshold of the house of death held particular importance. Significance was also attached to other thresholds, for example, when in Scotland a 'bidder' went out to invite relatives and friends to the funeral, he or she did not cross the threshold of those invited but delivered the message across it (SSS Archives: Bidding). In many districts, visiting mourners were greeted at the threshold of the house of death by the chief mourner, given a glass of alcohol (wine or ale) or a cup of tea, and a verbal greeting exchanged. In some places the greeting was as ritualized as the encounter; for example, in Northern Ireland it took the form of the phrase: 'I'm sorry for your trouble' (McCracken 1979). The visit would be continued with a formal visit to the body, and often a farewell involving kissing or touching the body, usually on the brow, a ritualized invasion of the body's physical boundary which seems to have reinforced the importance of the gesture (DDD:23-6).

In some areas of Britain, particularly in Wales, these visits would most commonly be made for the wake on the eve of the funeral. Noisy wakes – scenes of 'Sport and Drinking and Lewdness' – were suppressed in Wales over the course of the nineteenth century, a process which probably occurred earlier in England (DDD:12-13). The idea appears to have been to celebrate the dead person by inclusion in a final social gathering, which aside from the feasting and drinking consciously involved the creation of light and noise. Lit candles were kept by the body during the watching period, warding off the dark. It is said that – as in the case of church and other bells – the noise was held to disturb the atmosphere and confound or ward off evil spirits. A similar idea may be behind the curious custom of shooting guns into the air at military weddings and funerals (DDD:26-7). Light and noise created a sort of *cordon sanitaire* around the body to protect it from evil spirits, and the boisterousness of the event also provided a comatose corpse an opportunity to awake. In districts where no eve-of-funeral wake was customary, visiting would be done on an individual basis during the period between death and burial, or more commonly on the day of the funeral itself, and feasting took place after the burial.

We now come to the day of the funeral, when knots on or near the body are said by some folklorists to have been loosened just prior to burial so as to facilitate eventual resurrection. Others record them as having been left tied, to prevent the spirit from walking (DDD:20). Coffins dating from the eighteenth and nineteenth centuries recently excavated from church crypts in the London region show evidence of knots *in situ*.* Whether this was due to a current belief in haunting or to the unimportance of the matter may never be known.

Farewells having been made, the coffin lid was generally nailed down on the day of the funeral, just prior to the final journey. An omen was attached to the sound heard out of context, which presaged a death

---

* Personal communication.

(Porter 1969: 27). The nailing-down process represents the rather violent transformation of an important threshold into a permanent boundary. The sound of the hammering may have been agonizing to many.

Because much folklore recording was done during and after the period in which grave robbery was widely feared (1750-1840), protection of the body from molestation after burial appears to have been an important consideration. Indeed, for a considerable period the size and number of coffin nails were a sign of status. In vault burial – which was believed more secure than traditional earth burial – people were usually buried in two or three coffins: wood, lead, and a further outer wooden case. Double and triple coffins must have been very heavy to carry, and some of the customary visiting and viewing was probably forgone if the body was already sealed in lead ready for the funeral. In the early nineteenth century patent iron coffins were manufactured, with special springs on the inner lid to prevent bodysnatchers from obtaining access. Many other methods were employed to protect the dead from molestation, burial of the whole body being considered a prerequisite for eventual resurrection (DDD:15-17).

A further matter of possible significance is that until the moment of nailing down, most of the customs associated with the body were home-based and largely female in character. Washing and laying out were traditionally done by women, as were the dressing and winding. Watching, too, was often a female activity, and the hospitality offered to mourners was provided by their labours. The eighteenth-century prints mentioned above show women taking customary roles indoors. The nailing down of the coffin lid was done by the coffin-maker or undertaker, and presaged the onset of the public and more male-dominated part of the proceeding: the funeral itself.

The process towards burial offered a sequence of boundaries, which codified and reinforced the process of parting: the sealing of the coffin, removal feet first; the journey; arrival and delivery to the grave. In the house, the first bearers would form up beside the coffin to carry it outside, either for a walking funeral or to bear it to a vehicle – hearse or bier. Crossing the threshold was crucial, as it had to be done feet first, and *never* by a back door (Addy 1895: 122; Baker 1974: 151; Radford 1961: 83, 168-9). Often this proved exceedingly difficult, particularly in small houses. Sometimes entire window frames were removed when small hallways or doorways would not permit a coffin its rightful exit. The feet-first position, so that the corpse would face away from the house of death, was said to encourage its spirit to do likewise, and for this reason it was thought to prevent haunting. For the rest of the journey the coffin was positioned in the same way. The intention appears to have been to reinforce the funeral as a one-way journey to disposal, deliberately designed to remain unidirectional.

In some parts of the country a prayer or service would be said at the threshold, or psalms or hymns sung. As we shall see in a moment, this process was occasionally repeated at significant places on the route to the grave, reinforcing the association of threshold, boundary and processional route (Gammon 1988: 412 ff.).

Once outside the house, the funeral procession would form up in an order of precedence. Nearest and dearest came first, with other male relatives being positioned as relief coffin or pall bearers, and then an ordering of close and more distant relatives and friends. The order of precedence was strictly dictated in heraldic funerals, but in most cases, the undertaker or the family would sort the rest out naturally. This is still observed to some extent today, when the undertaker's own cars carry the closest family and friends behind the hearse, while others follow in some order in their own vehicles.

It was widely considered bad luck to precede a coffin in procession (as it was to meet it, or to cross its path), but churchmen, heralds, and latterly undertakers seem to have accepted the risk and taken this position as the best one from which to 'conduct' the funeral to the grave (Radford 1961: 72). In many localities the coffin was 'conducted' by the undertaker walking before the coffin or hearse to the limit of the local community, a visible or invisible boundary (a road intersection or at the limit of five hundred yards or paces) being the cue for him to get on and ride the rest of the way (Richardson 1978).

Neighbours not attending the funeral would often stand by their own thresholds to pay respect to the neighbour leaving the district for ever, and in many places also observed the custom of lowering blinds or drawing curtains in their own windows on the day of the funeral (Richardson 1978). Often it would also be neighbours who looked after the house to prepare for the return of the mourners, remembering not to lock the door, which would have been an omen of further death or bad luck (Addy 1895: 123; Hole 1953: 223).

The journey to the burial place was not always direct, and was occasionally punctuated by a series of stops – either by slowing down or pausing for a moment, or by stopping altogether for refreshment, prayers or singing. These stopping sites could be linear or associational.

I have records of several accounts of funerals which took the form of a perambulation, eschewing the shortest route for a roundabout one which took in stops at the dead person's regular public house, or workplace, or some other site which had an association with the deceased (Addy 1895, 125; Hole 1940: 54). In a recent case the custom of perambulating the remains was adapted to cremated remains.*

---

* This case is discussed more fully in a paper on cremation which I presented at the Katharine Briggs Club in 1991, and which is now in preparation for publication.

Death's Door

In most older accounts linear stopping places were at topographical or natural boundaries, such as crossroads or rivers on the direct route. In the days of walking funerals, doubtless such stops provided much-needed periodic rests. However, as I suggested above, many customs serve more than one purpose, and it will be seen from the following extract from Dorothy Wordsworth's journal that more may have been going on than the simple provision of resting places, or pretexts for worship:

> They set the corpse down at the door, and . . . the men with their hats off sang with decent and solemn countenances a verse of a funeral psalm . . . When we came to a bridge, they began to sing again, and stopped during four lines before they entered the churchyard. (Wordsworth 1971: 3 Sept. 1800, 38)

This short extract features two thresholds – door and gate – and a bridge boundary. The halt at the bridge perhaps coincides with the recorded belief that evil spirits could not cross open water (Gammon 1988: 437; Brown 1979: 26, 66, 78).

In Wales every crossroad is said to have prompted a halt for prayers (Jones 1930: 214) while in the Highlands and Islands it was customary for each mourner to add a stone to a cairn at every resting place (SSS Archives: Cairns). Probably the best known linear marked route in southern England is that of the Eleanor Crosses, which commemorate the overnight resting places of the body of Queen Eleanor on its way to Westminster Abbey in 1290. The crosses' original sites were at road junctions: that at Charing Cross stood where the statue of Charles I now stands looking down Whitehall.

The evidence is inconclusive as to whether crossroads were considered safe and hallowed places because of their cruciform shape, or dangerous and unhallowed because they marked the intersection of boundaries, thus constituting a sort of no-man's land. Suicides were traditionally buried at such intersections, but later commentators are uncertain as to why this was so. Crosses were cut in turf at the site of fatal accidents or crimes, so it seems that the cross served to cleanse or attenuate bad associations while nevertheless perpetuating them (Puckle 1926: 153; Peacock 1895: 335; Radford 1961: 131-2). A similar sort of doubt lingers over the stopping places. Were these marked sites sanctified by contact with the dead, or rendered dangerous by it? Were they thought of as stepping stones for the spirit or consecutive barriers to its return? The idea of stopping places as stepping stones for a spirit to follow may bear some sort of relationship to the ancient Lyke Wake dirge, sung over the corpse between death and burial, which describes how to navigate the hazards of the post-mortem journey (Gammon 1988).

Bertram Puckle (1926) mentions that

... it was once considered necessary for the funeral procession to return from the graveside by a different way to that by which the corpse was carried, in order to render it more difficult for the departed shade to return.

Bruce Castle at Tottenham is said to have shown physical evidence of this custom. Its walls had apertures which had been specially made in order that funerals might pass through to the churchyard, which were subsequently bricked up (Puckle 1926: 158; Watford: V, 556). If Puckle is to be relied upon, the custom looks, like many others, to articulate uncertainty concerning the location of the departed spirit, and doubt as to whether it was friendly or hostile to survivors (DDD:17).

Certainly the idea that coffins had rights of way suggests that the body was held to change the route in some existential manner, and since a right of way benefits all the community, the change looks to have been regarded as a positive one – except perhaps by landowners (Puckle 1926: 122-3). The provision of what were known as 'bier balks' – unploughed paths across fields for use during the funerals of those dying in outlying hamlets or farms – also suggests that the needs of the dead and their bearers were accorded special respect in rural communities, needs which were popularly held to override any legalistic understanding of boundaries and land ownership.

Dorothy Wordsworth's reference to singing at entry to the churchyard in September 1800 (Wordsworth 1971: 38) brings us to the next important threshold in the funeral journey, the churchyard gate. The site is frequently gated and roofed over with a structure called a lych gate, or corpse gate. Here the coffin could rest a while for singing and prayer, and there too the churchman met the procession and assumed responsibility for the ceremonies leading to interment.

The aspect of entry of the coffin to the churchyard and church appears in some places to have been thought important. In Lincolnshire it is said to have been considered 'both indecent and unlucky for a corpse to enter the Churchyard by any avenue except the East Gate', and in the same region it is said to have been customary to enter the church for funerals by the north door (Howlett 1893: 137; Gutch 1908: 247). It is not known if these Lincolnshire observances relate to those of bearing a coffin sunwise around the church or churchyard recorded in north-east Scotland between the seventeenth and twentieth centuries. The east gate/north door route, interestingly, provides a sunwise circuit. The portrait of the Elizabethan diplomat Sir Henry Unton reads left to right, and his life, death and funeral are shown in a sunwise circuit.* However,

---

* Crombie MSS, Folklore Society Archive, London; Simpkins, J.E., *County Folklore* VII, 1912-14, p.170. The Unton portrait is now in the National Portrait Gallery, London.

Death's Door

lych gates are not uniformly situated to the east of churchyards: that at Coverham in the North Riding of Yorkshire provides a classic westerly example.* There is some evidence to show that the sunwise route was considered 'superstitious' after the Reformation, and disapproved of. Whichever entrance or exit was used, the corpse is still customarily carried feet first, and the popularity of orientation (face to the east) is widely recorded both in the folklore and in the east/west direction of graves in many churchyards (Addy 1895: 122; Puckle 1926: 148, 150).

The sacred building itself contains important thresholds and boundaries which are discussed in Canon Porter's contribution to this volume. It is worth observing, however, that the most expensive and highly valued sites for burial were within the church threshold (the nearer the altar the more prestigious) and that certain sectors of the churchyard were considered more or less advantageous. The north side, bounded by the church's shadow, was always considered an unhappy place, reserved for the unbaptised or the transgressor (Brand 1905: 286; Gutch 1908: 246).

The grave itself is the corpse's final threshold. The grave is often described as 'yawning' or 'gaping', which implies a consuming orifice, not unlike medieval images of the mouth of hell. Among the images which adorned seventeenth- and eighteenth-century funerary invitations were crossed spade and pick, which echoed the old custom of protecting the threshold by leaving implements crossed over the threshold until its use. It is my own view that the ubiquitous crossbones may derive from a similar custom associated with exposed human bones in churchyards. In pre-Reformation days the open grave was censed and doused in holy water by the priest in the form of the cross.† Today the starkness of the upturned earth at the threshold is softened in many municipal cemeteries by the use of green cloths in an attempt to render the sight of the freshly disturbed earth and cavity less upsetting (Nicholl 1991: 95).

The burial service being said, the lowering of the coffin across the final threshold reinforced its irrevocability. Surrounded by the mourners, only the coffin entered the grave. The evident weight of the coffin, the sound as it reached the bottom, and of earth on the lid, all conspired to make this the most harrowing moment of all. The pain and difficulty of the moment was traditionally mitigated, again, by the singing of popular funeral hymns, later suppressed by the Church (Gammon 1988).

The threshold of the grave was associated with a number of ritualized farewell gestures. During night funerals, popular in higher social spheres in the eighteenth century, torches would be extinguished by

---

* I am indebted to Robert Thorne for this information.
† Personal communication with K. Lacey, University of East Anglia.

being upturned into the earth surrounding the grave, and at the funerals of great aristocrats the staff of office would be broken at the graveside and buried with the coffin (Gutch 1908: 241; Radford 1961: 75-6). More commonly observed customs include the carrying by mourners of rosemary or other evergreens, which were dropped into the grave after the coffin. Flowers, too, were often strewn into the grave (Hole 1940: 57; Peacock 1895: 331; *Cheshire Notes & Queries* 1883: 3; Brand 1905: 239).

Once filled, the open threshold became a boundary several feet deep, whose surface was itself marked and bounded. The most widespread manner in past times was by the making of a long rounded mound over the grave with the excess earth, in a shape which served as an analogue for the buried body. In many churchyards these mounds were rendered formal and permanent by the later addition of stone mounds in the same shape, marked at head and foot, with vertical headstones carrying personal details, and footstones with usually only initials and/or death date.* The less financially fortunate used wooden graveboards, of which few examples survive.† We are all perhaps familiar with other types of burial plot marking in churchyards and cemeteries. Burials inside churches were marked with a flat slab or a raised monument over or near the body.

The extent to which the grave was regarded as a one-way threshold is, I think, evidenced in the sense of outrage expressed by entire communities when bodysnatching was discovered. Bodysnatching violated all the physical and symbolic boundaries we have discussed, and did so when the buried dead – and therefore also the grief of mourners – were at their freshest. The disturbance of graves was deeply disturbing. To preserve the inviolability of the grave, not only were watchmen set, but burial ground boundaries and thresholds were reinforced, as the high walls at Kensal Green and Highgate or the moat surrounding the Glasgow Necropolis bear witness. These fears were by no means confined to the vulgar: the Duke of Wellington was buried in four coffins (DDD:77-99).

In the same era the boundaries of grave spaces were reinforced: kerbs, railings and raised tomb markers became more widespread in outdoor burial. Such boundary markers are nowadays frowned upon by burial authorities, since they are inconvenient to powered lawnmowers. Older times would probably have viewed askance the institutionalizing of

---

* Many of these 'body' or 'mummy' stones still survive in old churchyards. One, at Westerham in Kent, is illustrated in B. Bailey, *Churchyards of England and Wales*, London, 1987, p. 114.

† Decayed graveboards are occasionally found in odd corners of churchyards. I photographed two surviving in the churchyard at Monken Hadley, Barnet, in 1977. One from Mickleham, Surrey, is illustrated in Bailey, op. cit. p. 117.

traffic over graves, as there was an interdict on walking on graves (Radford 1961: 173; Peacock 1895: 332). The extent to which the grave site was considered an analogue for the buried body, and indeed for the buried person, can only be hinted at here. Weed clearance, painting, the planting or the setting of cut flowers was often confined to the area within the grave's own boundary markers, or concentrated near the headstone. This is still very much the case today. Urban burials, being geographically distant from the parishes they serve, tend to be less well cared for – one reason cremation has been so eagerly adopted in our own century, particularly in urban districts.

The subject of cremation raises an important matter: the frequently expressed dissatisfaction many people ascribe to ceremonies at crematoria (Davies 1990: 23-4). One of the greatest problems with cremation is, in my view, the result of unsatisfactory thresholds, particularly in the last threshold which substitutes for the grave. The grave is a very final threshold, which when filled becomes a serious and permanent boundary. The threshold in cremation suffers because it does not accord with the threshold of the furnace: it is a *euphemism* for a final threshold, and is therefore unconvincing as a final boundary. To a large proportion of the public, the cremation threshold palpably fails in its necessary function of transforming a threshold into a permanent and convincing boundary (Ness 1991: 103-4).

The importance of funerary rituals for the health of the bereaved is now becoming increasingly understood. I have argued elsewhere that, if fully observed, many of the customs recorded over past centuries in these islands would go a long way towards assisting the soul by all known means, preventing premature burial, *and* most importantly, preventing the denial of death which so many observers have commented upon as a feature of our own era. Since the marking of boundaries and thresholds was such a significant feature of funerary customs in these islands in the past, it seems sensible to suggest that any revision of rituals or of funerary architecture should involve a reconsideration of their importance. The necessary processes of separation associated with the transformation of thresholds into convincing boundaries seem to me historically to have been profoundly important in laying the dead to rest, and thus providing real comfort to survivors.

REFERENCES

Addy, S.O. 1895: *Household Tales*. Sheffield.
Baker, M. 1974: *Folklore and Customs of Rural England*. Newton Abbot.
[Bewick, T.] 1962: *1,800 Woodcuts by Thomas Bewick*. New York.
Brand, J. 1905 (1777): *Observations on Popular Antiquities*. London.

Brown, T. 1979: *The Fate of the Dead*. Mistletoe Books 12. Folklore Society. Ipswich.
Davies, D. 1990: *Cremation Today and Tomorrow*. Nottingham.
Gammon, V. 1988: 'Singing and Popular Funeral Practices', *Folk Music Journal* V (4), 412-47. London.
Gutch, E. & Peacock, M. 1908: *County Folklore, Lincolnshire*. Folklore Society. London.
Hole, C. 1940: *English Folklore*. London.
Hole, C. 1953: *The English Housewife in the 17th Century*. London.
Howlett, E. 1893: 'Burial Customs', *Westminster Review*.
Jones, G. 1930: *Welsh Folklore and Folkcustom*. London.
McCracken, R. 1979: *Aspects of the Funeral in an Ulster Setting*. Sheffield.
Misson, H. 1719: *Mémoires et observations*, trans. Ozell. London.
Morley, J. 1971: *Death, Heaven and the Victorians*. London.
Ness, J. 1991: 'Facing Death', *Proc. Institute of Burial and Cremation Administration*. Conference at Southport. Derby.
Nicholl, M. 1991: 'Burials: Which Way Forward?', *Proc. Institute of Burial and Cremation Administration*. Conference at Southport. Derby.
Peacock, F. 1895: 'Traditions and Customs relating to Death and Burial in Lincolnshire', *The Antiquary*.
Porter, E. 1969: *Cambridgeshire Customs and Folklore*. London.
Puckle, B.S. 1926: *Funeral Customs*. London.
Radford, E. & M. 1961: *Encyclopaedia of Superstitions*. London.
Richardson, R. 1978: *Death in the Metropolis*. M.A. thesis.
Slack, P. 1985: *The Impact of Plague in Tudor and Stuart Britain*. London.
SSS Archives: School of Scottish Studies, University of Edinburgh.
Watford, E. n.d.: *Old and New London* (6 vols). London.
Wordsworth, D. 1971: *Journals of Dorothy Wordsworth* (M. Moorman ed.), London.

ACKNOWLEDGEMENTS

Without the generous encouragement of Hilda Davidson this paper would have not seen the light of day in time to appear in this volume. I should also like to thank the following for assistance given in researching this paper: Hilda Richardson, Brian Hurwitz, Judith Davis, Marija Anteric, Jean Tsushima and Vic Gammon. The British Museum Reading Room, the Folklore Society Library at University College, London, and the School of Scottish Studies, University of Edinburgh, have been invaluable sources of help and information.

Contributors

THEO BROWN
Formerly Folklore Recorder of the Devonshire Association and President of Folklore Section. Author of *The Fate of the Dead* et al.

DR HILDA ELLIS DAVIDSON
Formerly Vice-President of Lucy Cavendish College, Cambridge, and President of the London Folklore Society. Author of *Gods and Myths of Northern Europe, Katharine Briggs, Story-Teller* et al.

KARIN KVIDELAND
Theologian from Norway with an interest in folklore.

DR REIMUND KVIDELAND
Director of the Nordic Institute of Folklore, Turku, Finland.

DR PATRICIA LYSAGHT
Lecturer in Irish Folklore and Ethnology in the Department of Irish Folklore, University College Dublin.

SAMUEL PYEATT MENEFEE
Attorney and folklorist, with degrees from Yale, Oxford, Harvard and the University of Virginia. Author of *Wives for Sale*, winner of the first Katharine Briggs Prize.

PROFESSOR THE REVD CANON J.R. PORTER
Professor Emeritus of Theology in the University of Exeter. Formerly President of the Society for Old Testament Study, and President of the London Folklore Society.

DR RUTH RICHARDSON
Research Fellow of the Institute of Historical Research. Author of *Death, Dissection and the Destitute*.

Contributors

ALAN W. SMITH

Retired Headmaster, and sometime Hon. Secretary of the London Folklore Society. Author of *The Established Church and Popular Religion 1750-1850*. Currently researching on maritime themes.

DR JULIETTE WOOD

University of Wales Fellow 1986-88, working on a comprehensive type and motif index of Welsh folktales, to be published by Folklore Fellows Communications. Honorary Lecturer in the Department of Welsh at University of Wales College, Cardiff.